D0871007

EMPATHY, FANTASY and HELPING

Volume 65, Sage Library of Social Research

Sage Library of Social Research

Empathy, Fantasy and Helping

Ezra Stotland, Kenneth E. Mathews Jr.,
Stanley E. Sherman, Robert O. Hansson,
Barbara Z. Richardson

Volume 65
SAGE LIBRARY OF
SOCIAL RESEARCH

 SAGE PUBLICATIONS   Beverly Hills   London

Copyright © 1978 by Sage Publications, Inc.

All rights reserved. No part of this book may be reproduced or utilized in any form or by any means, electronic or mechanical, including photocopying, recording, or by any information storage and retrieval system, without permission in writing from the publisher.

For information address:

SAGE PUBLICATIONS, INC.
275 South Beverly Drive
Beverly Hills, California 90212

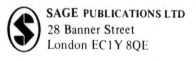

SAGE PUBLICATIONS LTD
28 Banner Street
London EC1Y 8QE

Printed in the United States of America

Library of Congress Cataloging in Publication Data

Main entry under title:

Empathy, fantasy and helping.

   (Sage library of social research ; v. 65)
   Bibliography: p. 117
   1. Empathy.   2. Fantasy.   3. Helping
behavior.   I. Stotland, Ezra, 1924-
BF575.E55E46   152'.4   78-5721
ISBN 0-8039-0984-5
ISBN 0-8039-0983-7 pbk.

FIRST PRINTING

CONTENTS

INTRODUCTION

[W]hole audiences at the current revival of 'Death of a Sales-man' at the Circle in the Square sit sobbing in unison, with every sign of thoroughly enjoying their miserable state. The same phenomenon was evident 25 years ago, when I first saw the play . . . .

"The skill with which the author manipulates our emotions is an enviable one . . . the fact is that the emotions of the play are not of the loftiest; they are exacted from us by a situation so pitiable that to fail to respond would be to bear witness to our inhumanity. Of *course* we feel a tearful sympathy for Willy Loman . . . and for his dull-witted, about-to-be-bereaved family. . . . As fellow-creatures, we dare not turn our backs on them or follow our in-stincts and look away, as we would from some dreadful accident in the street. At the same time, what we feel for them is the all too easy compassion that is a function of the sentimental view of life. . . ."

Brendan Gill, *New Yorker* (1975)

Is it *sympathy, empathy* or *emotional contagion* that leads whole audiences to weep when confronted with Arthur Miller's Loman family? In this familiar setting where the observable behavior of many individuals is similar, underlying processes may vary tremendously, but the process of most interest to today's psychologist would probably be *empathy*.

Empathy has been defined by one social psychologist who has done extensive research in the field (Stotland, 1969) as a state in which "an observer reacts emotionally because he perceives another experiencing or about to experience an emotion." Writing in the *International Encyclopedia of the Social Sciences*, another psychologist (Wispé, 1968) points out: "*empathy*, unlike *sympathy,* denotes an active referent. In *empathy,* one attends to the feelings of another; in *sympathy* one attends to the sufferings of another, but the feelings are one's own."

It can be assumed that some people in the audience of *Death of a Salesman* in New York's Central Park were empathizing— identifying in fantasy with one or more members of the cast and experiencing similar emotions. On the other hand, the *New Yorker's* theater critic, precise in his use of the English language, felt that his *sympathy* had been "exacted" from him. In this situation, at least, he was a nonempathizer.

It has long been recognized that a playwright who is skilled in his craft can create an emotionally charged situation and elicit empathetic responses from individuals in his audience. Within the last few years it has also been demonstrated that physiological responses correlated with emotional arousal can be elicited in the laboratory under controlled conditions of empathetic responding (Berger, 1962; Lazarus, 1966; Stotland, 1969; Stotland et al., 1971). Some of these experiments will be described in the pages that follow.

At least one question remains to be answered: Are some people more empathetic than others? The first laboratory studies of empathy carried out by Ezra Stotland and his associates at the University of Washington during the 1960s were aimed at reproducing the phenomenon of empathy and studying its determinants. The main focus was on varying the social relationships between the empathizer and the model. In more recent studies, to be described in this volume, a way was sought to predict individual differences in empathy and to demonstrate that empathy as a response tendency is general across situations. As a result of these studies, a promising instrument, known as the fantasy-empathy (F-E) scale, was constructed and validated.

The current interest among psychologists in empathy and sympathy has its roots in a wider movement among America's social scientists to broaden the scope of psychological investigation beyond the study of human aggression and related behaviors. The research emphasis on altruistic and pro-social behaviors, if it can be dated, could be said to start with studies of the Kitty Genovese murder in New York (Darley and Latané,

1968) and various studies and experiments on bystander intervention that followed. Clearly, empathy and sympathy are
intuitively attractive possibilities as mediators of altruism, but
it should be noted that the relationship between empathy and
helping behaviors is as yet undocumented.

Stotland's early work on empathy, which he termed "exploratory," was designed around predictions as to the effects of various
social relationships on empathetic responding; these predictions
were generated from social schema theory, a theory dealing with
the various cognitive structures that individuals utilize in their
perceptions of other people and social situations. It was hypothesized that ordinal position in the family is one determinant of
these social schemas and, as predicted, first and only children
tended to respond empathetically to people who differed from
them on the dimension of status, while later-borns related on the
similarity dimension, showing more emotional arousal when the
model was a peer or was perceived as similar to the self.

Because no differences in the total amount of empathetic
responding were found between first-and-only and later-born
children, the question of individual differences in empathy
remained for further study. When the F-E scale was later constructed (see Chapter 2), it was possible to use the measuring
techniques already developed in the laboratory for validation of
the scale. If, as early results now suggest, empathy is a general
behavior tendency for some, this too would fit in with a major
tenet of Stotland's social schema theory. The theory maintains
that to reduce anxiety in new and ambiguous situations, certain
individuals develop higher-order or generalized schemas about
the techniques of observing or imitating other people (Stotland
and Canon, 1972: 349). One oι these suggested schemas is that
playing the role of the other in fantasy is a good source of information. One of the results of such fantasy role-playing may be
self-instruction in taking the role of the other and feeling the
emotions the other feels.

Detailed experimental instructions on how to imagine what
one would feel in the place of another have been found to enhance
empathetic responses, as contrasted with the effect of instructions to watch the other's physical movements carefully (Sher-

man, reported in Stotland, 1969). A new finding, reported in this volume, is that in contrast to the "imagine self" perceptual set, general instructions that simply ask the subject to "empathize," i.e., to try to feel the same emotions as the model, are no more effective than instructions to try *not* to feel the model's emotions, and that neither of these two sets differs significantly from a condition of no instructions. In short, subjects have to be told explicitly how to empathize if they are to do so.

Armed with a scale to measure individual difference in empathetic responding and with techniques for measuring empathetic arousal in the laboratory, will researchers find a clear path from empathy to altruism? It seems unlikely. Initial experiments using the F-E scale, reported here, suggest that the relationship between empathy and helping behavior is a complex one, and perhaps curvilinear as in the case of the reported relationship between fear and attitude change. Although research on empathy is closely tied to the current work on altruism and pro-social behavior, it should be stated that Stotland's definition of empathy, quoted earlier, includes but is not limited to the matching of the perceived emotion of the other (Berger, 1962). Such a match is termed "simple empathy" (Stotland, 1969), but the theory also encompasses the possibility of "contrast empathy," i.e., a feeling of joy in the failure of a rival, etc. As yet, there is not much laboratory evidence for contrast empathy.

Finally, the experimental study of empathy is a new field. Much remains to be learned. Work on the F-E scale is described here in some detail in the hope that researchers will use and improve it. The devisers of the scale are grateful for the pioneering work of Alan Elms (1966) from whose scale to measure fantasy they drew two of the three F-E items. So far, additional items tested have failed to add to the reliability and validity of this scale, but its use in populations broader than the present sample of college students, nurses, teachers, and employees of social service agencies may produce additional valid items.

Chapter 1

THEORY AND RESEARCH ON EMPATHY

Empathy, where the emotions of one person call out emotional responses in others, is a process in human interaction that is central to social psychology. This reaction can occur in any interpersonal setting, and something similar can also happen when people watch a play or read a book.

Theories dealing with the related concepts of sympathy and emotional contagion can be traced back to the beginnings of philosophical thought, but the term empathy was not introduced into the English language until early in this century. It was to be 50 years before the first laboratory studies of empathy began to be reported in the 1960s.

Cornell psychologist Edward B. Titchener, an Englishman who represented the German tradition in America, is credited with the first use of empathy in English as a translation of the German word *einfühlung*. Titchener outlined for American readers the theories of German psychologist Theodore Lipps, who envisioned a state of aesthetic empathy in which the perceiver loses self-awareness as his identity becomes used with the object he is observing (Boring, 1957). The American social psychologist William McDougall (1908) used empathy to describe something quite different—a primitive process of emotional contagion. In succeeding years, definitions of empathy have continued to vary widely.

Because the present volume will focus on empathy as a basic process in interpersonal relations and on the individual characteristics of the empathizer, it is important to start with our own definition. This view of empathetic responding will be contrasted with theoretical definitions of the concept of empathy currently in use in psychotherapy and psychoanalysis, in cognitive approaches to child development, and in personality assessment. The second part of this chapter will describe laboratory research on empathy, which began in the 1960s: studies of altruistic responding, and experiments on the effects of the social context on empathetic responses.

The research reported here and in succeeding chapters is based on, or interpreted by, a definition of empathy drawn from Stotland (1971): "An observer reacting emotionally because he perceives that another is experiencing or about to experience an emotion." The meaning and measurement of emotion is crucial here. Also important is the *direction* of the influence: this definition would exclude both *projection,* where the observer attributes his own feelings to the model, and *labeling,* where the observer uses the model's behavior for a cognitive definition of his own physiological reactions. Stotland's definition of empathy allows for the possibility of any type of responding emotion in the observer. As philosopher Max Scheler (1954) has pointed out, empathy is not a reproduction of another's experience. The flavor of the emotional response will be colored by the personality of the observer and by factors in the interpersonal situation.

While the emotion of the observer who is empathizing can never be exactly the same as that of the person he is watching, it may often be similar. When the responses have the same valence—positive to positive or negative to negative—the process is described as "simple empathy." This is the kind of response that is most commonly referred to in discussions of empathy. The definition quoted above also includes the possibility of contrasting emotion, where the response is positive to negative or negative to positive. Sadism as well as altruism can thus be encompassed by the definition.

The cues of emotion which elicit empathy can be of various types. Aronfreed (1968) distinguishes between overt expressions of emotion in the observed person and situational factors which are assumed to cause the emotion. Response to cues of the first type he calls *empathy* and response to cues of the second type he terms *vicarious reaction*. Such a distinction is difficult to support empirically. Researchers in the field of person perception (see Tagiuri & Petrullo, 1958) have consistently reported that people tend to rely on knowledge of another's situation to judge the other's emotional experience. Thus, what Aronfreed calls a vicarious reaction is often the basis for an empathetic relationship. In the experimental studies to be reported, subjects perceived another to be experiencing an emotion because of the laboratory situation the other was in. In the empathy process, as conceptualized here, the observer assumes an emotional response in the other based on a variety of cues. It is this perception, a perception that elicits an emotional response on the observer's part, that we call empathy.

From the vantage point of psychotherapy, Katz (1963) has described the empathetic relationship between therapist and patient. The first person experiences the feelings of the other "as if they were his own." Katz suggests that the process is not completely under the control of the empathizer and that a person cannot empathize deeply at will, but can only free himself to allow it to happen. Katz also stresses the existence of individual variations in the level of empathy, and suggests that "something other than situational factors" must account for such differences.

On the other hand Carl Rogers (1967), another psychotherapist who sees empathy as important in the client-therapist relationship, emphasizes cognitive understanding rather than emotional involvement. "To sense the client's inner world of private, personal meanings as if it were your own, but without ever losing the 'as if' quality, that is empathy."

Psychoanalytic theory stresses the affective quality of the empathetic process, which is viewed as a consequence of the mechanism of identification as delineated by Freud. Fenichel (1945) defines empathy as consisting of two steps: "(a) an identification with the other person, and (b) an awareness of one's own feelings after the identification and in this way an awareness of the object's feelings." Nevertheless, Eikstein (1972: 80) has stated that "full identification will destroy empathy. Empathy is a kind of in-between stage, a sort of temporary identification; it is the most important tool of the psychotherapist who is to understand his patient, to identify with him temporarily on a trial basis, but who must maintain his own identity."

Empathy was seen by Sullivan (1953) as being very important in the personality development and socialization of the young child. Through empathy the infant can feel and be affected by the attitudes and emotions of significant people even before it is able to understand the signs of emotional expression. Whatever the mother's emotional feelings are, the child is sensitive to them. Anxiety and rejection in the mother create reciprocal anxiety and insecurity in the child. Likewise euphoria and approval in the mother elicit positive feelings in the infant. Empathy is emotional communication which cannot be defined in ordinary language. How this process occurs is not made clear.

Sullivan's view of empathy is in sharp contrast to that of present-day cognitively oriented theorists in the field of child development. Many of these researchers, working in the tradition of Jean Piaget, see empathy as a form of social cognition, a mature or nonegocentric stage in the process of cognitive development. Attainment of this stage involves role-taking skills and the understanding of complex social situations (Piaget, 1932; Flavell et al., 1968; Borke, 1971; Chandler and Greenspan, 1972; Iannotti and Meacham, 1974; and others). Norma Feshback (1973) has pointed out the problems with this viewpoint: "When empathy is defined solely in cognitive terms, it has little theoretical utility beyond that contributed by the cognitive functions themselves. More important, a strictly cognitive definition neglects . . . its affective dimension."

The same criticism can be applied to other cognitive approaches to empathy based on the role-taking theories of Mead (1934). Researchers in this tradition (see Cline and Richards, 1960; Rogers, 1957; Dymond, 1950; Hatch, 1962; Kerr and Speroff, 1951; Mahoney, 1960) define empathy operationally as accuracy in predicting another person's thoughts, feelings, and behaviors. Consequently, in practice, they tend to view neutrality and detachment as important characteristics of the successful empathizer. This approach is exemplified in the scoring of Dymond's (1949) scale to measure "predictive empathy," the first of a number of similar instruments. Furthermore, this approach to the measurement of empathy has been severely questioned on methodological grounds. As a number of critics have noted (Cronbach, 1955; Gage and Cronbach, 1955; Hastorf et al., 1955), the correspondence between predicted and actual ratings and/or behaviors can be due to a number of factors not measured by the test, including projection or role familiarity.

A final approach to empathy defines the concept within the framework of the profession of therapy. Here it is assumed that the therapist's empathy can be measured by judges' ratings of actual samples of his or her behavior during interactions with another person. The first test to use this technique and still the most widely used is Truax's (1961) accurate-empathy (A-E) scale, which defines empathy as "both the therapist's sensitivity to current feelings and his verbal facility to communicate this understanding in a language attuned to the client's current feelings" (Truax and Carkuff, 1967). Tape recordings of short segments of actual therapist-patient interactions are randomly selected and rated by judges (usually undergraduate students) who are naive in regard to therapy or therapeutic theory. The judges are trained for a period of several hours to distinguish between nine levels of A-E and then are asked to rate the therapist's A-E from the taped segments of the interviews.

One valid criticism of Truax's test is that empathy is confounded with skill in communication. In addition, there are methodological and interpretative difficulties with this scale.

For example in a factor analytic study of A-E ratings that used only five levels instead of nine levels, Zimmer and Anderson (1968) identified eight factors, which accounted for 73 percent of the total variance in the ratings, an unlikely result if the A-E scale were measuring a unitary construct which varied along a single continuum. Other critics in reviewing A-E research suggest that the A-E scale is measuring some more global aspect of therapist behavior than the definition suggests, and that inappropriate statistics have been used to demonstrate reliability. They add that the A-E scale does not have discriminant validity in relation to Truax's own scales of genuineness and nonpossessive warmth. Other critics point out that A-E ratings for therapists are similar regardless of whether A-E raters are allowed to hear clients' statements or not, and that "proof" of the scale is derived from either face validity or outcome studies using subjective patient and therapist evaluations of therapy effectiveness. (See Shapiro, 1969; Chinsky and Rappaport, 1970; Rappaport and Chinsky, 1972.) Because of the severe definitional and methodological issues raised concerning the accurate-empathy scale, the usefulness of this measure is suspect.

To sum up, until the 1960s the concept of empathy was theoretically rather than empirically defined. The original definition is based on affective responding. As expressed by Stotland, empathy is a process where "an observer reacts emotionally because he perceives that another is experiencing or is about to experience an emotion." In recent years other approaches have equated empathy with a variety of social skills in person perception and communication, but these theories lie outside the scope of the research to be reported here.

Experimental Research on Empathy

Laboratory research on empathy began only in the last two decades, and the literature is not extensive. Several experimental programs in the 1960s reported here involved empathetic responding to films and models, although the finding were not presented by the investigators as empathy research. Next are described experiments on altruistic responding, which were based on the assumption that an empathetic process triggered the behavior measured, although the investigators did not attempt to measure empathy. Finally, in the experiments on the effect of social context on empathy, we see empathy and its physiological correlates measured in the laboratory.

Responding Empathetically

Lazarus and his associates did a series of experiments designed to study the physiological symptoms accompanying psychological stress, in which subjects' reactions to movies showing physical pain were measured. In the first study (Lazarus et al., 1962), heart rate, skin conductance, and Nowlis mood ratings were compared for a bland film on farming and for a movie on aboriginal subincision. This was a silent film which showed a series of crude surgical operations on the male genitals of adolescents as performed by the people in a native culture of Australia. It was found that the physiological and subjective responses to the subincision film showed markedly more arousal than those to the film on farming. Furthermore, the skin conductance responses followed closely the high and low tension points of the subincision film.

A second study (Speisman et al., 1964), used only the subincision film. Three sound tracks were devised, representing various observational sets. In the "trauma" condition the sound track stressed the pain and mutilation shown, in the "denial" condition it was suggested that no pain and danger existed in the minds of the adolescents portrayed, and in the "intellectualization" condition the comments followed the detached attitude of the anthropological observer of strange customs. Subjects exposed to the latter two sound accompaniments showed significantly lower physiological stress reactions as compared to a control group shown the original silent version.

A further study (Lazarus et al., 1965) employed the same paradigm, but used another film showing a series of accidents in a wood mill, and again it was found that instructions either stating that the events were not real but only dramatizations or suggesting that subjects adopt an impersonal orientation sharply reduced physiological stress reactions as compared with the silent version.

Although Lazarus and his associates were not ostensibly studying empathy, experimental convenience dictated the use of films as stimuli. This created conditions for the study of vicarious reactions to stress, a process that can easily be interpreted in terms of empathy. Furthermore, a study by Alfert (1966) experimentally evaluated the vicarious threat from viewing a film, as an analogue to the process operating in direct threat. Subjects either viewed the wood mill film without a sound track or heard instructions that threatened them with receiving painful electric shocks. The correlations found between physiological reactions to direct and vicarious threat were substantial.

One aspect of the Lazarus studies of particular interest to empathy theorists is his use of the traditional psychological defenses of denial and intellectualization as independent variables. The effectiveness of instructions to viewers to deny or ignore film cues suggesting physical pain seems to underscore various ways in which individuals can minimize the empathy response.

EMPATHY RESPONSES TO MODELS

Berger (1962) used a classical conditioning paradigm to demonstrate that empathy can occur in the laboratory. He called the process "vicarious instigation" when the observer responds emotionally to a performer's unconditioned emotional response. In Berger's first study, male subjects in the experimental condition watched a model who was ostensibly receiving an electric shock to his arm after a warning signal. Each time a light dimmed and a buzzer sounded the model jerked his arm back in response. A control group observed the model jerk his arm, but these subjects were not told he was receiving a shock. As predicted, Berger found more frequent galvanic skin responses (GSR) in the test trials of the experimental (shock-movement) condition. In a second study (DiLollo and Berger, 1965) two more control groups were added: shock-nonmovement and movement-no shock conditions. Again the shock-movement group had significantly faster reaction time to the dimming light and buzzer in the test trials.

Berger's important finding of greater vicarious instigation in the shock-movement condition suggests that it is the combination of vicarious and empathetic cues that creates the strongest stimulus, rather than the simple addition of cues to a stimulus configuration such as an extra dial or light. This interpretation is strengthened by the work of Tomes (1964), a study similar to Berger's in which the experimenter conditioned GSR responses to subjects watching a model receiving shock. Tomes found that a combination of stimuli including signal devices indicating shock was being administered and appropriate responding by the model enhanced empathy. He also found that when subjects themselves experienced shock immediately prior to the experimental manipulation, empathy was *not* enhanced. This latter finding suggests that recent experience with the stimulus is not necessary for empathy.

In another study demonstrating empathetic reactions in the laboratory through use of a classical conditioning paradigm, Bandura and Rosenthal (1966) investigated the effects of manipulated emotional arousal on vicarious conditioned GSRs to a tone that preceded the delivery of shock to a model. Emotional arousal was varied by drug injections, placebo injections, and the threat of expecting to change places with the model. Of particular interest here were the self-reports of subjects on the post-experimental questionnaire. With a few exceptions, subjects described strong empathetic reactions to the model's pain, including some instances of sadistic satisfaction or "contrast" empathy. Furthermore, a number of subjects described strategies designed to reduce the aversiveness of the vicarious instigation procedure that required them to witness another's pain—strategies which suggest the manipulations used in the Lazarus film studies described above. These included focusing the eyes on a spot distant from the model's face and hands, looking across the room or out the window, thinking about academic problems, planning a trip, or concentrating on a love affair.

EMPATHY AND ALTRUISTIC RESPONDING

Aronfreed and Paskal (Aronfreed, 1968) approached empathy from the point view of associative learning. Working with children in a series of experiments involving both positive and negative experiences, these researchers demonstrated that six- to eight-year-old girls can learn to press a lever that will give an adult a pleasurable experience in preference to pressing another to obtain candy for themselves, and they can also learn to reduce the pain of another child.

In the first study subjects in the experimental group learned to press a level activating a light in preference to a lever producing M & M candies. These altruistic subjects received affection from the adult experimenter, who also showed pleasure each time the light came on. In one of the two control groups the adult showed pleasure at the onset of the light and in the other gave affection when the light came on. In Aronfreed and Paskal's second study, children in the experimental condition first heard a loud, painful noise through earphones; three seconds later the adult experimenter showed evidence of hearing the noise. Next, the children heard the noise again and were taught by the experimenter to press a lever to turn it off. In the test phase, another child wearing earphones showed distress signs as if hearing a noise. For control subjects either the temporal association of their hearing the noise and the experimenter's pain was random in the first phase, or the noise turned off by the experimenter in that phase was not a painful one. Subjects who had been in the experimental condition in the first phase were more likely in the test phase to turn off the noise that was presumably causing distress to the other child. In other words, those subjects whose pain had been associated with that of the experimenter acted altruistically.

Aronfreed and Paskal did not measure empathy in any of these experiments, but they did assume that an empathetic process occurred in the experimental conditions of both the pleasure and the pain studies. In other words, they assumed that in each case the child had learned to feel an emotion of pleasure or pain by association with another's expressed emotions.

Two recent studies in an instrumental conditioning format lend support to Bandura and Rosenthal's (1966) suggestion that the empathetic pain from watching another receive shocks can be aversive. In the first of a series of three experiments replicating an earlier study and based on an escape conditioning paradigm, subjects of Weiss et al. (1973) viewed another individual performing a motor task and showing overt signs of stress at regular intervals from supposedly painful shocks. Subjects' ostensible task was to observe the other person and press a series of buttons to "record" their observations. In the experimental group, subjects were led to believe that their button pressing terminated the shock, whereas in the control group no effect was apparent. Over a series of 15 trials the "altruistically reinforced" experimental group learned the instrumental response as measured by starting speed in the button press, whereas the control group showed no learning.

The results of Weiss et al. on reaction time in relieving a model's pain were replicated in a study by Geer and Jarmecky (1973), which also measured physiological responses of observers. Subjects were all male undergraduates who came to the laboratory for an experiment called "interpersonal problem solving under stress." They arrived to find a female confederate, ostensibly another subject, in the waiting room, and then they were led to believe that selection of the woman for the "stress" condition a little later was by chance. Experimental conditions included high and low shock to the model and opportunity or lack of opportunity for the observer to throw a switch to terminate each shock. Not only was reaction time faster when the subject had an opportunity to terminate the shock, as in Weiss et al. (1973), but it was also faster when the subject believed the model was receiving a high level of shock. Physiological data supported the assumption that empathetic arousal was present, with significantly more spontaneous skin conductance responses in the stress condition in which the subjects believed the model was receiving a high level of shock.

THE EFFECTS OF SOCIAL CONTEXT ON EMPATHY

While the investigations described above have shown that empathy can be demonstrated in the laboratory, these researchers did not investigate the effect on empathy of different types of interpersonal relationships. It is in this area that Stotland has focused his work (Stotland, 1969; Stotland et al., 1971). This research was conducted in a laboratory which was used in some of the studies to be described in the next two chapters. The general procedures will be outlined here. (See Appendix A for a more detailed description.)

The typical paradigm employed in these studies is that of a number of subjects, usually five or six, observing another person, who is usually a pseudo-subject and trained assistant, while this person is undergoing either a positive or a negative experience. The emotional reactions of the observers are usually measured by two of three physiological indicators—palmar sweating, rises in basal skin conductance, and vasoconstriction, as well as by subjects' ratings of their own feelings. (See Appendix B for details of measurement.)

Subjects are instructed by the experimenter that they are participating in a study of "the process of social observation as it occurs in small groups with a minimum of information." They are seated at tables on which the apparatus for measuring physiological responses is set up. They face the front of the room and a table on which are placed a diathermy machine and a large separate dial on which all controls and readings are easily visible.

The paid assistant is always selected from among the real subjects, supposedly by chance, to be the model or "demonstrator" on the diathermy machine. Subjects are told by the experimenter that the machine can be set on three levels of intensity: low (pleasant reaction), intermediate (neutral reaction), and high (painful reaction). The level for each session is randomly selected to minimize experimenter effects.

The paid assistant sits in a chair with his back to the subjects[1] and performs different body movements for each of the three levels of heat registered on the dials. Physiological measurements are taken at set intervals during the procedure, and the subjects' reports of their own feelings are rated on seven and nine-point scales immediately after termination of the emotionally arousing stimulus to the person with whom they might empathize. (See Appendix C for rating scales.)

The hypothesis that a basic element in the process of empathy is the imaginative self-involvement of the observer was one tested by Stotland and Sherman using this procedure (Stotland, 1969; Stotland et al., 1971). It was predicted that, if the observer were instructed to imagine either how the other person was feeling or how he himself would feel in the other's position, the observer would empathize more than if the instructions were to be concerned merely with the other's outward appearance and actions.

Before the diathermy machine was turned on in this experiment, subjects received one of three sets of randomly distributed instructions concerning what they were to do when they subsequently watched the demonstrator undergo the "treatment." In the "Watch Him" instructions, the subjects were to attend to the demonstrator's physical movements only, e.g., his head or arm movements. In the "Imagine Him" instructions, the subjects were to imagine how the demonstrator felt and what his sensations and thoughts must be. In the "Imagine Self" instructions, the subjects were to imagine how they themselves would feel if they were the demonstrator and what sensations and thoughts they would experience.

The results showed that in general the subjects manifested relatively high emotional arousal when the demonstrator was perceived to be in pain, provided they had received either of the two "Imagine" instructions. They reacted less after receiving the "Watch Him" instructions. When the treatment was perceived to be neutral, the variations in instructions made little difference as measured by the subjects' reactions. When the treatment was perceived to be pleasurable, there was also little evidence of empathy. In short, subjects empathized more when they imagined how the other person felt or imagined themselves in his position, provided it was painful. Thus, the perceptual set a person takes in viewing the other affects the degree of empathy.

This same experimental setting was used by Stotland and his associates to investigate the kind of interpersonal situations that serve to enhance empathy. The "Imagine Self" study just described suggests that other interpersonal situations which tend to make a person imagine how the other person feels will also enhance empathy. One such interpersonal situation is that involving high perceived similarity between the self and another. It was found (Stotland, 1969; Stotland et al., 1971) that high perceived similarity did, in fact, increase empathy, but almost exclusively for people who were later-borns rather than first-borns or only children. In these studies perceived similarity was experimentally varied by a variety of means: personality as measured by tests, having experience on the same experimental task prior to the empathy situation, similarity of status, and others. In further studies it was found that later-borns empathized more with someone with whom they had interacted, even if the interaction had been purely in the form of a game with no substantial communication. Later-borns also empathized more than first-borns under conditions in which achievement motivation had been aroused. There were other situations in which first-borns and onlies empathized more, including those in which the other person was either above or below them in status as opposed to the same status level. Still other studies in the series concerned the effects on empathy of fear arousal, envy, success, and failure.

A recent study by Krebs (1975) also demonstrated the effect on empathy of perceived similarity or dissimilarity with a performer. Similarity was manipulated by the instructions via reported scores on personality tests. Half of the subjects in each similarity group believed the performer was experiencing monetary rewards and painful shocks while playing a roulette-like game, and the other half that the observer was participating in a motor-conceptual task. Physiological responses of the observers were monitored as they watched the performer go through a series of "conditioning trials," based on Berger's (1962) paradigm, and subjects in the high similarity group, who were led to believe the observer received rewards and punishments, showed significantly more skin conductance responses than those in the other three experimental conditions. Measurements of heart rate and vasoconstriction, however, did not differ among groups. In a final trial all subjects were given the opportunity to make an altruistic response by rewarding the performer at a cost to themselves. Subjects in the high similarity-reward/punishment condition who had shown more skin conductance also scored significantly higher on a scale indicating willingness to receive shock and give up monetary reward to the other than did subjects in the other three groups. No birth order data were reported in this study.

None of the experimental studies described so far were designed to predict individual differences in empathy. Birth order differences emerged from Stotland et al.'s analysis (1969; 1971), but the effect of this variable appeared to be that of determining which type of social relationship would enhance empathy. Nevertheless, the fact that the effects of different interpersonal situations on empathy were mediated by birth order, an individual difference variable, suggested a new direction in research on empathy—a direction to be described in the chapter that follows.

NOTE

1. The demonstrator did not face the subjects for the practical reason that it was not feasible to train student assistants to do a convincing job of expressing feelings facially. This procedure also served to minimize variations in expression over experimental sessions.

Chapter 2

ADDING A NEW TOOL: DEVELOPMENT
OF SCALES TO MEASURE EMPATHY

Reporting research by Stanley Sherman
and Ezra Stotland

Empathy as a human process, an emotional contagion that can occur whenever two or more people meet and communicate, was the focus of the laboratory studies carried out by Stotland and his associates and reported in Chapter 1. The researchers viewed empathy as a process shaped by all the variables of the social situation including the status, perceived similarity, and previous interaction of the participants, as well as by the personal orientation of the empathizer—this person's expectancies and aroused emotions. These, then, were the variables manipulated in the experiments that were carried out.

AUTHORS' NOTE: This study was made possible by a National Science Foundation grant to Ezra Stotland.

Another approach to empathy is feasible. Few of us have failed to note that some people are sympathetic and warm in all their social interactions, while a few seem totally insensitive to the feelings of their fellows. Social psychologists studying person perception have theorized that this warm-cold personality dimension is central to the way individuals organize their impressions of other people. Do some people have a greater capacity to empathize with others—an empathetic personality trait?

This question and others that arose during the course of the experimental research on empathy led Sherman and Stotland to take a new look at the problem of individual differences. It was becoming apparent that a deeper understanding of empathy as well as better predictions could result if the problem were studied directly.

Some questions that concerned the researchers were: (1) To what degree should empathy be thought of as a general trait that varies among people and to what degree should it be considered a specific response to a certain stimulus for each person? (2) Are some people characteristically empathetic in a contrast way, that is, do some feel a positive emotion when the other is feeling a negative emotion? (3) Do some people always experience simple empathy, that is, feel the same emotion as the other is expressing? (4) Do some people empathize more with negative feelings than with positive, or vice versa? (5) How does empathy relate to other personality variables that have been studied?

To explore these questions studies were begun with the goal of developing a reliable and valid self-report scale to measure individual differences in empathy. Initially, a number of personality scales that purported to measure "empathy" were examined, but none was found that was designed to deal with the individual's capacity for emotional or affective experience, that is, with the transfer of emotion from the perceived to the perceiver that Stotland defines as empathy.[1]

The research plan developed by Sherman and Stotland sought to answer the questions raised above by discovering what kinds of empathetic experiences seemed to group together. The first step, then, was to administer a number of test items to an appropriate sample and to study the relationships through further analysis. To obtain relevant items from the widest possible range of social situations and relationships, a mapping procedure was developed, based on the laboratory research on empathy described in Chapter 1. The map (Table 2-1, Appendix D) consisted of a hierarchy of 36 categories of situations where empathy might occur.

The first differentiation in the mapped hierarchy deals with the quality or sign of the emotion that the empathizing person perceives in the other: this can be either positive or negative. On the second level is the observer's responding emotion, which can be either similar or contrasting. Relationships between the observer and the observed constitute the third level of the hierarchy, and here three possible relations were explored: similarity, liking, and dependency. Finally, the fourth level involves another facet of the empathizer's perception of the other, the perceived cause of the observed person's emotion. Three categories are listed here: physical cause (e.g., pain from the diathermy machine), achievement (e.g., success in a test), and social success.

While these causes on the fourth level were felt to cover much of the broad range of causes of human emotion, the social situations in level three were only a small sample of possible relationships, and it should be emphasized that the researchers recognized that there are other ways of conceptualizing situations where empathy could occur. It was nevertheless hoped that this hierarchy would be useful in developing a fairly representative set of test items.

Items were constructed in a systematic way to represent each of the 36 cells in the schema. The representation was not perfect, as a number of cells had two items and some cells had none. Eight items of a more general nature were constructed which did not seem to fit clearly into any cell, and several items were borrowed from Elms' fantasy-empathy scale (Elms, 1966). The 48 questions in the first draft were structured in Likert form, giving the subjects five options of agree-disagree. These items, put in random order together with 37 fillers, were administered to a group of 32 junior college students. Based on the responses of these students, six items were dropped for lack of variance and more filler questions were added.

This revised questionnaire was then presented to two large psychology classes at the University of Washington totaling 576 students (224 males and 292 females) and the results were subjected to an orthogonal factor analysis using the varimax method of rotation (Kaiser, 1958). Factor scales were formed using items which had a loading of .40 or more and six factors were derived from the analysis. (See Tables 2-5 through 2-10, Appendix D for the items in each factor.)

Factors two through six were clear-cut and independent, and only two items in these five factors loaded above .40 on more than one factor. The first factor scale appeared to be a response bias, in that the 12 items loading on it were the last 12 items in the empathy scale.[2] Factor one was therefore discarded, and using factors two through six, five empathy scales were constructed and are described below. (See Tables 2-5 through 2-10 in Appendix D for complete list of items in each factor.)

Denial-Avoidance Scale. Factor two could be said to reflect a defense or resistance against empathy. The highest loading item here is "I seldom get deeply involved in the problems and experiences of others." The scale appears to express a refusal to empathize.

Involvement-Concern Scale. Factor three items all indicate simple empathy. Several questions reflect involved concern for the condition of others. The highest loading item on this factor is: "When I see a retarded child, I try to imagine how he feels about things."

Hostility-Empathy Scale. Factor four, which is correlated .31 (p < .02) with factor two, seems to be a clear representation of contrast empathy. The highest loading item on this factor is: "Sometimes I'm not at all pleased when I hear about a person who got top grades." The important difference between this scale and factor two appears to be that the theme of factor two is refusal to empathize, while most of the items on this scale express empathy in contrast form.

Friend-Empathy Scale. Factor five is correlated .53 (p < .01) with factor three, and is also a measure of simple empathy. Most of the items refer to empathy with friends. The highest loading item is: "When a friend becomes engaged or gets married, I am very happy."

Fantasy-Empathy Scale. Factor six has only three items, and they all concern the idea of involvement with an important character in a story, play, or movie. The highest loading item is: "When I am reading an interesting story or novel, I imagine how I would feel if the events in the story were happening to me."

Since construct validation has not been completed on all these scales, it is pointed out that the names used must be arbitrary and cannot be construed as adequate descriptions of the dimensions measured.

Before beginning the validation process on the five scales, a second factor analysis was done on a new sample of 154 subjects who were also students in an introductory psychology class. While the factors found were a little different, the same basic structure held. On each factor the items expressed either simple or contrast empathy. For the few exceptions to this the items had negative loading on the factor. Again, therefore, the most important dimension was simple or contrast empathy. In this analysis there was also a strong tendency for the items on a given factor to reflect a specific area of concern, either social, achievement, or physical. All other dimensions were randomly distributed on the factors. It was decided to employ the factors of the earlier analysis because it had the larger group of subjects, the factors had good face validity, and there were no negative loadings.

How effective was the mapping procedure, which was designed to obtain a wide and fairly even distribution of items carrying the experience of empathy? First, it should be noted that the factor analysis supported only to a small degree the a priori classification structure used to guide the writing of items. On the other hand, two important distinctions did appear in the factor structure: those between empathy as opposed to nonempathy and those between simple empathy as opposed to contrast empathy.

Taking the levels of the hierarchy in order: on the first level, items describing positive or negative emotions of the observed person loaded indiscriminately on all factors except factor two (denial-avoidance). In general, people who report they empathize when a person is happy also report they empathize when the person is sad.

The second level, concerned with the emotions of the observer, which are either similar to or opposite to the emotions of the observed, discriminates simple empathy from contrast empathy. This distinction was upheld by the factor analysis. The true contrast items all loaded on factor four (hostility-empathy scale). Some items written to express opposite emotion (i.e., with contrast empathy in mind) also suggested noninvolvement, and they ended up in factor two.

The third level in the hierarchy, relationship between the observer and the observed, was not supported by the factor analysis. Persons who reported they empathized in one of the three types of relationship (similarity, liking, and dependency), also said they empathized in the others.

The final level was the area of the perceived cause of the emotional experience of the person observed, an area divided into physical, social, and achievement. Here there was some support for the classification. While items of these types were fairly well scattered on all the factors, achievement items were clustered in factor four (hostility). This factor, representing contrast empathy, included five achievement items and one physical item.

It is possible that an analysis containing a much larger pool of items separated into many more factors might support more of the distinctions made by the schema. In any case, the important distinctions found in the analysis were between simple empathy as measured by factors three, five, and six; contrast empathy as measured by factor four; and nonempathy as measured by factor two. For all practical purposes, it seems clear that the most important question is whether a person reports that he or she empathizes or not. If the report is affirmative, empathy will be expressed in many types of situations. Thus, the factor analysis is consistent with the concept of empathy as a general overall response tendency or trait as opposed to a set of distinctive responses to specific stimuli. Although the general response tendency does not account for all the variance in individual differences, the factor structure suggests that it is an important determinant.

Factor scale scores for all subjects were computed by giving five points for each item answered by "strongly agree," four for "agree," three for "not sure," two for "disagree," and one for "strongly disagree." The total points were then summed for the scale. A higher score means the subject describes himself as having more of the quality represented by the scale. Mean scores and standard deviations on each scale are shown in Table 2-2, Appendix D.

As with all self-report devices, the self-concept of the individual can be assumed to play an important part in his or her empathy test score, because a person's self-picture may include a rather general awareness of being empathetic or nonempathetic. This will not be perfectly correlated with the way the person feels and behaves in specific situations. The role prescription for females includes empathy to a greater degree than does the male prescription, and on each of the five scales female subjects scored about two points in the direction of more empathy than males. These differences are small but stable and significant. Table 2-2 (Appendix D) shows the means on each scale for males and females, together with the t tests and significance levels. While this finding fits in with the popular notion that females are more empathetic than males, it is not clear whether females are truly more empathetic or merely tend to see themselves this way. It may be that both are true.

Scale means were also compared for two separate birth order breakdowns and for a birth order by sex split. No significant differences were found. In Stotland's laboratory studies of empathy, birth order differences were found, but it should be pointed out that each of these empathy scales contains many types of empathy situations. With global measure, birth order groups may well have an equal tendency to empathize. It is the very specific stimuli which elicit birth order differences in the Stotland studies—stimuli which are assumed to arouse specific social schemas or expectations. For example, Stotland et al. (1971) have presented data which indicate that a later-born responds sympathetically to people who are similar to him more often than first-borns or onlies do. Because of the way the questions in the empathy scales are phrased and because of the way they clustered in the factor analysis, this schema of similarity could not become a dimension useful in differentiating birth order subjects.

VALIDATION OF SCALES

Two types of validity information were obtained for the five empathy scales—predictive and construct data. The first approach was to assess the predictive ability of the scales by correlating scores of individual subjects with their physiological responses and their self-reports in a laboratory experiment on empathy. A validation study was designed for this purpose, following the procedure of the experiments by Stotland et al. reported in Chapter 1 (see also Appendix A).

Forty-nine subjects were chosen for the validation study, based on their scores on two of the simple empathy factor scales: the involvement-concern scale (factor 3) and the friend-empathy scale (factor 5). The two scales were used together in this manner because the factors correlated .53 ($p < .01$) for the entire sample of 576 subjects, and were thus viewed as measuring similar processes. Twenty-seven subjects who scored more than one standard deviation above the mean on either factor scale (15 males and 12 females) were designated as high empathizers. Twenty-two subjects who scored more than one standard deviation below the mean (11 males and 11 females) were designated as low empathizers. Males and females participated in separate sessions of the experiment with same-sex models.[3]

The validation study, then, had a 2 x 2 design, high and low empathizers, male and female. Subjects were told that they were participating in a study of the process of social observation and were tested in small groups. They were seated at a table facing the diathermy machine, and the demonstrator, a paid assistant, was ostensibly chosen by chance from the group. Subjects were told that the machine could be set on any of three levels of intensity, but when the experimenter picked up the card from his desk to announce the "randomly selected" level of intensity for the session, it was always the high or painful level. This procedure was followed because the pain condition had elicited the strongest response in the earlier experiments. While subjects observed the demonstrator at the machine, measures of their physiological reactions were taken. Later they responded to a series of items in laboratory questionnaires, describing their feelings during the experiment.

Measurements were thus taken on three physiological dependent variables, vasoconstriction to the announcement of the heat level and to the turning on of the diathermy machine and palmar sweat during the entire demonstration. The fourth dependent variable was the subjective report on the laboratory questionnaires. Subjects who scored high on the empathy scales could thus be compared with low scorers using four laboratory measures. T-tests were made between the means of the four measures to compare the performance of the high and low scoring groups, called high and low empathizers. This was the major analysis for the validation study. It was also possible to make a secondary analysis of the data by computing correlations between the subjects' laboratory responses and their empathy scores on the denial-avoidance scale, the hostility-empathy scale and the fantasy-empathy scale. These correlations were appropriate analyses because these three scales had not been used to select subjects for the experiment, and scale scores were normally distributed for the sample population.

It was possible to obtain some further validity information from data available from two other laboratory experiments which had used essentially the same format as the validation study but which had included manipulation of additional independent variables. In one case the independent variable was perceived oppositeness of personality: 29 female subjects in this experiment had also previously taken the empathy scales. In the other case the independent variables were measures of perceived status and fear: here 22 male subjects were available. Both of these experiments have been previously reported (Stotland et al., 1971).

The results of this predictive validity research will be reported separately for each scale, summarizing the finds from all three experiments that relate to the scale. It should be noted clearly that the results are reported only in the form of *t* test analyses for the involvement-concern and friend-empathy scales in the validation experiment. All other results are reported in the form of correlation coefficients between scale scores and laboratory performance measures.

SIMPLE EMPATHY SCALES

Fantasy-Empathy Scale. When the data from the validation study on the three simple empathy scales were analyzed, only the fantasy-empathy scale yielded any significant results on the physiological variables in the appropriate direction. This scale is concerned with the degree to which people become involved with the actors in a play or the characters in a book. Here there was a significant correlation with vasoconstriction to the announcement of the heat treatment ($r = .29$, $p < .05$) and there were some nearly significant relationships with the laboratory questionnaire. High fantasy subjects indicated that they had imagined more how the demonstrator felt while he was going through the treatment ($r = .24$), and that they had imagined more how they would feel ($r = .25$). They also said they were more tense after the treatment ($r = .27$), and finally they showed more interest in getting to know the demonstrator ($r = .33$). In the oppositeness of personality study there was a near-significant correlation with vasconstriction to heat ($r = .24$), and in the questionnaire subjects indicated they had strongly imagined how the demonstrator felt during the treatment ($r = .63$) and how they would have felt if they had gone through it ($r = .51$). They also reported feeling more calm once the demonstration was over ($r = .39$). These questionnaire relationships are all significant to at least the .05 level.

The involvement-concern scale was not related to any of the physiological measures in the three experiments except for an almost significant correlation ($r = .29$) with palmar sweat in the oppositeness-of-personality study. On the post-experimental questionnaire in this same study high scorers felt the model was receiving more pain ($r = .29$), reported themselves to be feeling more tense just before the machine was turned on ($r = .33$), felt worse while the machine was on (r = .32), and felt they would have experienced more pain if they had received the treatment (r = .27). They also said they observed the model more carefully (r = .38). With 27 df all but the last of these correlations are less than significant but there is a consistent and expected trend throughout the data.

The friend-empathy scale also was not related to the physiological measures in the predicted direction. However, on the post-experiment questionnaire of the validation study high scorers felt the demonstrator's experience was more painful (t = 2.38), said they felt worse about it (t = 2.52), reported imagining how the demonstrator felt (t = 1.86), and that they observed his movement more closely (t = 2.92). The third and fourth comparisons only approach significance while the others are significant beyond the .01 level. Likewise in the oppositeness-of-personality study, using correlations, high scorers said they felt worse when they heard about the treatment (r = .31), and they felt more tense just as the machine was turned on (r = .45). Also in the status-fear study the scale was related in the predicted direction to vasoconstriction at the moment the machine was turned on (r = .58, p < .01).

The denial-avoidance scale was not significantly related to any of the physiological dependent variables in the validation study. In the laboratory questionnaires, however, high deniers reported being more relaxed while watching the demonstrator receive the pain treatment (r = .29) and after the treatment (r = .35). They also said they imagined less how the demonstrator felt (r = .33), imagined less how they would feel in his situation (r = .42), and they showed less interest in getting to know him (r = .33). With 47 df all of these correlations are significant at least p < .05.

In the oppositeness-of-personality study, which of course was limited to female subjects, there was a strong correlation with palmar sweat (r = .60, p < .01), indicating that high deniers sweat more watching the treatment. This finding is unexpected. At the same time they said the model received less pain (r = .44), and that they felt less bad and more relaxed when they heard it was to be painful (r = .33). They also felt less bad during the treatment (r = .34), imagined less how the model felt (r = .36) and how they would feel in her place (r = .30), and finally they reported observing her less closely (r = .29).

In the status-fear study, with all male subjects, the high deniers vasoconstricted less to the turning on of the machine (r = .48, p < .02) as would be expected. While high deniers consistently reported the predicted lack of empathy on the post-experiment questionnaire, the physiological data are in conflict. In the oppositeness-of-personality study high denying females unexpectedly showed more arousal while high denying males in the status-fear study showed the predicted lower arousal. The most straightforward interpretation is to accept the face validity of the scale that it measures avoidance of empathy, though it is possible that the females are denying their own feelings and reporting a lack of involvement when in fact they are experiencing emotional response.

The final empathy scale is best described as hostility-empathy. This measure was correlated with palmar sweat in the validation study (r = .33, p < .05). The more strongly subjects endorsed this scale, the more they showed palmar sweat. More hostile females described themselves as tense and nervous right after the demonstration (t = 2.24, 2.67 p < .05). The males, however, did not show this difference.

Likewise in the oppositeness-of-personality study the scale was correlated with palmar sweat (r = .37, p < .03). There is thus clear evidence that subjects who relate to others in a way that is flavored with hostility do show stronger involvement and are more aroused. In Stotland et al. (1971) other instances were found in which palmar sweating appeared to indicate hostile involvement with others.

In the oppositeness-of-personality study high scoring subjects felt the model received less pain (r = .37); their hostility was also revealed in their feeling the experimenter had done a poor job (r = .36) and their admission they had not tried to do their part too well (r = .28). Further, they evaluated the study as more unpleasant (r = .36). As in other experiments, this response in a pain condition has been interpreted as positive empathy in that the subject did not like the experience of watching someone endure pain. Here it might well be interpreted as an expression of anger against the experimenter and the whole experiment for inflicting such treatment on an innocent person. The hostile subjects are saying in effect: "We don't like it and we won't cooperate."

CONSTRUCT VALIDATION

The second approach to validation of the five empathy scales was a beginning attempt to evaluate the constructs defined by the scales. This was done by correlating the scales with a series of personality measures administered to the same subjects by Irwin Sarason.[4]

Sarason's questionnaire consists of 300 true-false items and is titled The Autobiographical Survey. It is routinely administered to most of the introductory psychology students at the University of Washington at the beginning of each quarter. It consists of ten personality scales primarily concerned with various manifestations of anxiety and hostility and including a measure of need-achievement and Edwards' social-desirability scale.

A total of 516 subjects of the 576 who responded to the empathy scales had also taken the Sarason survey. All the correlations between these measures reported are statistically significant at least at the $p = < .05$ level (see Tables 2-4, Appendix D.)

Correlations with the Sarason personality scales for the two factor scales that did *not* express empathy are described below. To a large extent these correlations upheld the researchers' analysis of the constructs these scales represent.

Denial-Avoidance. Statements such as "I seldom get deeply involved in the problems and experience of others," and "I feel other people ought to take care of their own problems themselves," loaded high on factor two, which seemed to express a denial or avoidance of empathy.

This scale was correlated with only two of Sarason's scales, in both cases in a negative direction. These were a scale measuring general anxiety and the anxiety-in-event-of-hostility scale, which measures the fear of what might happen if one becomes angry and aggressive. These correlations suggest that those who score high on the scale avoid both involvement and the anxiety associated with involvement.

Hostility. A strong flavor of hostility and contrast empathy is reflected in scale four, which includes such items as "sometimes I'm not at all pleased when I hear about a person who got top grades," and "I am pleased when a person who has beaten me in a game gets beaten himself." As noted earlier, high scorers on this scale were tense during the validation experiment and demonstrated significantly greater palmar sweat than low scorers. In the self-report questionnaires they downgraded the experiment.

The hostility scale correlated with more of Sarason's ten scales than any of the other empathy measures. Not surprisingly, there was a negative relationship ($r = -.17$) with Edwards' social-desirability scale, indicating the willingness of these subjects to admit hostility and dislike. The scale was also negatively related to a measure of defensiveness ($r = -.24$), which is endorsed by subjects trying to put themselves in a good light. There were positive correlations with four scales, three of them measures of hostility (general hostility, attitudinal hostility, and behavioral hostility), and finally a positive correlation with the lack-of-protection scale, which is an expression of childhood insecurity.

It is possible to shed some light on this set of correlations by considering some data gathered in the questionnaire used in the validation experiment. Hostile subjects described their home life as being more frustrating in high school and at the present time. Females also said there were more family conflicts during high school and at the present time than did low scorers. It seems, then, that this way of relating to people is partly related to the kind of family relationships a person has, and when there is conflict and tension in the family, people may be less ready to empathize in a simple and direct manner.

As noted, in the oppositeness-of-personality study, female high scorers on the hostility scale implied they rejected the experiment and did not try to play their part in it. The correlations with Sarason's scales support the interpretation that for those high on hostility-empathy, the empathy process is modified and colored by feelings of jealously, resentment, and desire to get even. In the laboratory for both the validation and oppositeness-of-personality studies the subjects became aroused in response to the treatment, but the tone of their feelings was not completely clear in the subjective data from the questionnaires. While they were showing anger toward the experimenter and the situation, their attitude to the demonstrator was not revealed. This factor scale measures hostility, but it has yet to be shown that it measures contrast empathy in its pure form.

SIMPLE EMPATHY SCALES

Not surprisingly, all three of the simple empathy scales were significantly correlated with Sarason's measure of anxiety when hostile. As noted earlier, all these scales were correlated in the validation experiment with interest in other people and ability to make friends. High scorers were more likely than low scorers to say they wanted to get to know the demonstrator. The correlations between these three measures are substantial: $r = .53$ between involvement-concern and friend empathy; $r = .38$ and $.25$ respectively between those two and fantasy-empathy. It was speculated that these correlations represent a high value placed on friendly personal relationships, which might be threatened by hostility.

The 14 questions on the anxiety-in-event-of-hostility measure refer to a fear of what might happen if one expressed anger, and also to a tendency to become disturbed while watching a display of violence. Typical is: "I get into arguments although at the time I regret my participation in them." The high scoring individual on this test is described as one who cannot tolerate interpersonal conflict because it is too threatening. Both because of his self-expectations and because of what others might think of him, he must "keep the peace" regardless of his feelings. Personal relationships are very important and not perceived as hardy enough to withstand clashes, so the high scorer must be sensitive to the feelings of others.

Involvement-Concern. Statements such as: "When I see a retarded child, I try to imagine how he feels about things," or "When I see a very old person, I often wonder how I would feel if I were he," are typically endorsed by high scorers on factor three. This scale correlated with four of the Sarason scales. The positive relationships were to the lack-of-protection scale (representing childhood insecurity) and to anxiety-in-event-of-hostility. There were negative relationships with the defensiveness scale and the social-desirability scale.

Friend-Empathy. High scorers on the fifth factor endorsed such statements as, "When a friend becomes engaged or gets married, I am very happy." Except for the positive correlation with anxiety-in-event-of-hostility, the friend scale was correlated only with Sarason's general anxiety scale. This correlation was in a positive direction, indicating that high scorers are willing to admit they are anxious. It may be noted that high scorers on the denial-avoidance empathy scale were significantly low on this general anxiety factor.

Fantasy-Empathy. The fantasy scale (factor six) includes such statements as: "When I am reading an interesting story or novel, I imagine how I would feel if the events in the story were happening to me." Scores on this scale correlated with only one of Sarason's personality scales, the measurement of anxiety-in-event-of-hostility.

SUMMARY OF VALIDATION RESULTS

Of the three simple empathy scales, the fantasy scale was related most consistently to the physiological variables and to some of the positive subjective reports. This is the more striking because this scale includes only three items, and the total possible range in scores is only 12 points. The scale also has substantial test-retest reliability. Mathews (unpublished) administered it to 45 students in an introductory social psychology course (16 females, 29 males) along with a number of other scales. Subjects were told that the tests were to be used for screening potential subjects in later experiments. Seven and one-half weeks later, the fantasy-empathy scale was readministered to 33 of the original 45 subjects who were present in the class. Subjects were told to fill out the scale as they felt it represented their feelings at the moment. The Pearson product-moment correlation was .83 (p < .01).

The results of the validation studies on the fantasy-empathy scale suggest that the dimension of fantasy or the ability to transplant oneself by imagination into another setting is an important contingency for the process of empathy. The imagine-self experiment (see Chapter 1) was another expression of this process, indicating that subjects can be instructed to adopt a set of imagining themselves in another's position, and this set apparently makes the other's experiences more vivid and real, so that the subjects react more to the stimuli impinging on the other. The F-E scale focuses on the use of this set as an individual difference variable.

Two of the three items in the fantasy scale were orginally drawn from a ten-item questionnaire by Elms (Elms, 1966) for research on the effects of role-playing on attitude change. The Elms scale also includes items referring to how much one imagines what others are thinking that are not included in the F-E items. In Elms' study, subjects who smoked were paid to participate in an experiment where they role-played telling a friend they had stopped smoking for specific health reasons. Elms found that his fantasy scale correlated .69 with a questionnaire reporting attitude change three weeks after the role-playing experience. Subjects with high fantasy ability changed their attitudes more after the role-playing experience. On the basis of these results, one might speculate that the tendency to fantasize in this way made the experience of role-playing more vivid and real to the subjects and in this way created more attitude change toward the feelings temporarily adopted in the experimental role.

The experimental results of both Elms' study and those described earlier lend support to the hypothesis that the perceptual set of imagination is one of the fundamental processes facilitating empathy and making it a more vivid experience for the observer or role-player. These first results in measuring the validity of the F-E scale suggest further that this set varies among individuals and that these variations can be measured.

EMPATHY AS A PERSONALITY CONSTRUCT

In evaluating the results of the work on the empathy questionnaire, there is evidence to suggest that empathy is a meaningful personality construct. The factor analysis is consistent with the notion of empathy as a general overall response tendency or trait, as opposed to a set of distinctive responses to specific stimuli. There is also support for this from the pattern of correlations resulting from the validation process for the five empathy scales.

In the factor structure, the most important distinctions that appeared were between empathy and avoidance of empathy on the one hand, and simple empathy and contrast empathy on the other. In addition, the fact that items referring to both positive and negative emotion are found on most of the scales suggests that people who empathize with positive feelings also empathize with negative feelings.

It is clear that of the five scales derived from the factor analysis, the fantasy and hostility empathy scales had the most solid support from the physiological data, and each also suggested a type of response which had been elicited at other times by independent variables in the laboratory.

The tendency to fantasize vividly the experience of others was shown here to be a fundamental part of the empathy process, as evidenced by the validity of this brief fantasy scale. This conclusion fits in with results of the study described in Chapter 1 where subjects empathized because they were given a preparatory set to imagine how the other person was feeling.

The role of the element of hostility, envy, or revenge in the empathy process merits further study. The scale derived from the factor analysis which has been labeled hostility or contrast empathy is correlated with three of Sarason's hostility scales, and high scoring subjects show high arousal in the laboratory but verbally reject the experience of an empathy experiment.

In conclusion, more information is needed to understand the relationship between the physiological and verbal levels of emotional response.

NOTES

1. Since development of the Sherman-Stotland scale, one such measure has been reported. See Mehrabian, A. and Epstein, N. "A measure of emotional empathy." *Journal of Personality 40*, 1972: 525-543.

2. It is possible that the response bias was created by pressure to finish the test, and some may have adopted a yea-saying or nay-saying set. It was impossible to find a common thread or meaning running through the items. Six of the 12 items loaded .40 or more on some other factor.

3. All subjects were drawn from introductory psychology classes, but because the validation study was run in the quarter following their class, these subjects were given one dollar in appreciation for their time. Only two subjects who were contacted declined to participate.

4. Some validity data have been reported on these measures (Sarason, 1958).

Chapter 3

THE ROLE OF INSTRUCTIONS:

FURTHER VALIDATION OF THE

FANTASY-EMPATHY SCALE

Reporting research by Dennis Mitchell, Ezra Stotland,
and Kenneth E. Mathews, Jr.

People who scored high on the fantasy-empathy (F-E) scale, as
reported in the previous chapter, empathized more than other
subjects in experimental situations in which they observed a
person undergoing a painful experience. One explanation for
this finding is furnished by Stotland's theory of social schemas
(1971, 1972). This theory hypothesizes the existence of learned
cognitive structures that guide behavior, and suggests that for

AUTHORS' NOTE: This study was made possible by a National Science Foundation
grant to Ezra Stotland.

certain individuals an existing schema may be aroused in social interactions that causes them to seek information by identifying with the other person and imagining what his thoughts and feelings are. In other words, such individuals may often give themselves instructions to play the role of the other in fantasy, and to feel what the other feels.

Experimental evidence has also been reported that when subjects in the laboratory are given explicit detailed instructions to imagine themselves in the other's position and to feel what the other is feeling, this imaginative role-taking enhances empathy (Stotland and Sherman, reported in Stotland, 1969). A question that still remains to be explored is whether, in the absence of such detailed instructions, a simple *decision* by the subject to empathize would enhance emotional arousal.

The question of just how detailed instructions must be is relevant to both laboratory and clinic. For example, an alternative explanation for the results of the Stotland et al. (1971) studies would have been the result of what has been termed demand characteristics or experimenter effect (Orne, 1962). It was argued that subjects might have interpreted information supplied to them, such as information that they were similar to the demonstrator or model, as an implicit demand to empathize. Furthermore, outside the laboratory, in clinical work, the assumption is often made that it is desirable for the therapist to empathize with patients (Rogers, 1957). Could a therapist simply decide to empathize without actively imagining himself in the other's mind? Would a decision to empathize enable the counselor to "sense the client's inner world as if it were (his) own?" (Rogers, 1967.)

To clarify the role of instructions in laboratory experiments on empathy, an experiment was designed and carried out by Dennis Mitchell, Ezra Stotland, and Kenneth E. Mathews, Jr. at the University of Washington. Another objective of the study was to further validate the F-E scale by comparing the empathy responses of low and high fantasizers. Two main hypotheses were: (1) When subjects are told to empathize, they will empathize more than when not so instructed; and (2) high fantasizers as measured by the F-E scale will empathize more than low fantasizers.

Notices on campus bulletin boards and ads placed in the campus and local newspapers were used to recruit 72 male subjects, who were paid $5.00 to participate in the two sessions of the study. The majority of the subjects were students, who participated in groups of four, five, and six. The laboratory and general type of procedure were the same as described in Chapter 1, except that only two settings of the diathermy machine were described and administered: the neutral or mild heat condition and the painful condition.

During the three minutes used to obtain a baseline measure of palmar sweat, the experimenter passed out instruction sheets for the subjects to read. The first part of the sheet contained a further description of the diathermy machine. The last paragraph of this instruction sheet always began:

> As stated previously, the condition used in a given session is randomly selected, and is unknown as yet even to the experimenter. Whichever condition is selected, the treatment lasts for only 20 seconds and has no permanent mental or physical effect on the subject.

The last sentence of this paragraph differed among subjects, depending on which of the three variations of instuctions the subject had been randomly assigned to receive, as outline below:

> *Empathize:* "While the heat treatment is being administered, your job will be to try to experience the same type of emotions as the person receiving the treatment. As much as you can, you are to try to feel what he is feeling."
>
> *Avoid Empathy:* "While the heat treatment is being administered, your job will be to try to *avoid* experiencing the same type of emotions as the person receiving the treatment. As much as you can, you are to try to keep yourself from feeling what he is feeling."
>
> *No Instructions:* In this condition nothing further was added to the last paragraph of the instructions.

When subjects had had an opportunity to read the instruction sheets, the experimenter picked up a card and announced to the subjects whether the painful or neutral condition was to be run. The subjects' vasoconstriction was measured at the moment they learned of the condition. Twelve seconds later, the machine was "turned on" (actually, of course, it was inoperative) for 20 seconds while the paid assistant acted consistently with the ostensible treatment. Each subject's vasoconstriction was measured again at the time of the turning on of the machine. Palmar sweat was recorded for the total period beginning with the announcement of which treatment was to be used at that session and ending about three minutes later. During the last two minutes of this period, the subjects filled out a questionnaire describing their experiences. In short, the design of the study included two levels of heat treatment, neutral and painful, and three different sets of instructions.

A week later, 62 subjects[1] returned for a second session to fill out the F-E scale as well as other personality measures. The study was then explained and the subjects paid.

An analysis of the data on both palmar sweat and vasoconstriction showed significantly more response in the pain condition than in the neutral condition, an indication that in general, subjects were displaying empathy. For palmar sweat the difference between the two conditions was signficant at the level of $p < .005$ (F = 11.41), and for vasoconstriction, $p < .025$ and $< .05$ (F = 7.30 and 5.60).

Instructions had no effect on a given subject's degree of empathy, which was inconsistent with the first hypothesis. There were no significant differences among the three instruction conditions on either of the physiological measures, and there was no interaction among the conditions.

High scorers on the F-E scale, consistent with the second hypothesis, empathized more in the pain condition than in the neutral condition as measured by palmar sweating. The correlation between F-E scale scores and palmar sweating was .37 ($p < .05$) in all three of the pain conditions pooled, while it was —.15 (not significant) in the three neutral conditions pooled.

No significant correlations were found between the F-E scale and the measures of vasoconstriction. There were no significant correlations between the F-E scale and items on the questionnaire about how subjects felt during the experiment. However, there was some tendency for the high fantasy subjects in the heat condition to report feeling more tense while the diathermy treatment was being given than did the low fantasizers.

While these results add support to the hypothesis that high fantasizers empathize more than lows, they give no indication that previous studies using a similar paradigm were biased by implicit instructions to empathize with the model or demonstrator. Also the results do not support the hypothesis that subjects will empathize as a result of being told to do so. Comparing this study to the Stotland and Sherman imagine-self study reported in Chapter 1, we can infer that a person needs to be instructed in *what to do* in order to empathize, that is, to imagine how the other person feels. This inference is supported by the finding in that study that people who instruct themselves to do this imagining tend to empathize more than those who do not, at least in a situation involving a painful experience where empathy is measured by palmar sweating.

Although there was a significant difference in vasoconstriction readings in the heat condition as opposed to the neutral condition, scores on the F-E scale were not correlated with vasoconstriction. This is somewhat puzzling in view of the significant correlations found between F-E and vasoconstriction in the validation study reported in Chapter 2. Because the results in this study on instructions parallel those in early laboratory studies (Stotland, 1969), a possible explanation is that the palmar sweating measure is sensitive to any emotion-arousing process that starts at any time in the three-minute period of measurement, while the two vasoconstriction measures are sensitive only to reactions which start at the time the measurement is taken. This may not coincide with the start of the imagining process. Because the procedure in the validation study was similar to the instruction study, it is not clear why the results on the physiological measures were inconsistent.

In any case, the results of this study on instructions provide an important element in the construct validation of the fantasy-empathy sscale, that is, the factor of discriminant validity. The significant correlation between the F-E scale and palmar sweating was found only in the condition where the model was exposed to painful heat. No relationship between fantasy and palmar sweating was found in the neutral condition. This is good evidence that the F-E scale is not a measure of sheer arousability or psychological responsiveness, but rather that it is measuring individual tendencies to respond physically to the perception of another's pain.

N O T E

1. Ten subjects failed to appear for the second session, and of those who did return, the records of two had to be discarded because of equipment failure in the first session.

Chapter 4

"MRS. REYNOLDS NEEDS A NURSE"

Reporting research by Ezra Stotland
and Kenneth E. Mathews, Jr.

In the experimental laboratory where Stotland and his associates did their studies on physiological correlates of empathy in social interactions, real models, ostensibly chosen from among the assembled subjects, were always used. It was in this setting that the first studies on the validity of the fantasy-empathy (F-E) scale were performed (see Chapters 2 and 3). Would the scale predict empathy outside the laboratory? And would high fantasizers empathize with characters portrayed in a film?

To answer these questions, a study was designed and carried out by Stotland and Mathews, using as subjects sophomore

AUTHORS' NOTE: This research was supported by a grant from the National Science Foundation to Ezra Stotland. Thanks are due to Clifford Lunneborg and Carl Jensema for their help with the statistical analysis.

nursing students at the University of Washington. The students were observed while watching a standard training film in which a hospital patient suddenly dies. The film, which is routinely presented to enrollees at the nursing school, is entitled, "Mrs. Reynolds Needs a Nurse."

Another purpose of the study was to examine some of the implications of the observed relationship between imagination and empathy. It has often been pointed out (e.g., Katz, 1963) that empathy is enhanced if an individual has had experiences similar to those of the other person. This may be so because the imagining process is facilitated by the person's recalling his or her own experiences. Empirical support for this is furnished by a study by Stotland et al. (1971) in which some subjects were led to believe that they would be the "demonstrators" on the diathermy machine. While these subjects sat waiting for the possibly painful experience they expected to have, they were no doubt imagining what this experience would be like. Then the experimenter informed them that he had made a mistake and that they would not be the "demonstrators." It was found that when they subsequently observed someone else undergo the painful treatment, these subjects empathized more than did other subjects who had not been led to imagine how they would feel as demonstrators. In other words, having previously imagined oneself in someone else's position increased empathy with that person. It would therefore be expected that a person who actually had had an experience like another's would empathize relatively more, because it would be easier for such a person to imagine himself or herself in the other's position.

Following this logic, nursing students viewing the training film could be expected to empathize more with the patient portrayed if they had been sick more, if they had had contact with sick relatives, or if they had had a death in their immediate families.

The general procedure in the film study was to measure the palmar sweating of nursing students while they watched the training film. Then, at the end of the film, the subjects rated their feelings while watching, indicated how much contact they had had with hospitals and illness, indicated their birth order, and filled out the F-E scale.[1] Subjects in the study were 127 sophomore nurses who viewed the film in the regular sessions of their fundamentals of nursing class. The students met in five sections, ranging in size from 12 to 50.[2]

The film, "Mrs. Reynolds Needs a Nurse," lasts approximately 40 minutes. It opens with scenes showing the nursing staff in a hospital ward getting organized for a busy day. The head nurse is a very efficient, businesslike person who quickly gets things under control. The charge nurse, who also serves as narrator of the film, is a warmer, more motherly type. Into this busy, over-crowded and overworked ward comes Mrs. Reynolds, a very fearful, elderly person with a serious lung disease who is wheeled in by her equally fearful and solicitous husband. Because no room is available, Mrs. Reynolds is placed temporarily in the hallway, thus initially presenting a problem for the nursing staff. She and her husband both demand a great deal of attention from the staff, which the staff gives only grudgingly with great annoyance and bitterness. This continues even when Mrs. Reynolds is placed in a room for an extended hospital stay. The husband complains to doctors and administrators, while the hospital staff attempts to demonstrate to the administrators that Mrs. Reynolds demands an exorbitant amount of attention.

Into this unhappy situation comes a young nursing student full of ideals and concern. She reacts sympathetically to Mrs. Reynolds' demands, but is disturbed by the hostility the regular staff displays toward this patient. She communicates her feelings to the charge nurse and then to the staff, pointing out that Mrs. Reynolds' demandingness is a consequence of her great fear of death. The staff responds by beginning to treat Mrs. Reynolds in a more reassuring, supportive way and by involving her husband more directly in the treatment process. Mrs. Reynolds' and her husband's attitudes to the staff change markedly for the better, and she shows general improvement. Suddenly, while watching TV, her head drops. The young student nurse rushes to her side and calls a doctor, who pronounces her dead. The staff are deeply upset by her death, and the film ends.

On the day of the test showing, the senior author of the study, Stotland, appeared in the classroom and was introduced by the regular instructor. He told the class he was going to do some research on their reactions to the film they were about to see. After indicating that they could participate in the research if they wanted to, he instructed them in the use of the apparatus to measure palmar sweating, which had been placed on each subject's table or book rest. This apparatus was somewhat different from that used in previous studies. It consisted of the following: a jar of acetone with ferric chloride in solution, some Kleenex, two cotton daubers, and a castinette-like gadget. The latter consisted of two flat pieces of wood stuck up against one another, and held together by rubber bands at one end. On the inner surface of one were attached two pieces of paper, which had been treated with tannic acid. The subjects first cleaned the pads of their index finger with the Klennex tissue, then daubed their pads with the acetone solution, using the cotton dauber. (The acetone quickly evaporates, leaving a residue of ferric chloride.) The subject then placed the castinette on her finger, one of the papers being held flush against the pad of her finger. The subject kept the castinette on for three minutes. The darkness was measured later by a photometer, just as in the previous studies.

The palmar sweat measure was administered for the first time before the film started to provide a baseline measure. The film was then shown up to the point about five seconds before Mrs. Reynolds dies, a point at which there was a natural break in the flow of the film. At this point, the lights were turned on and the subjects were instructed to place the castinette on their forefingers, using the second sheet of paper attached to the castinette. As soon as the castinettes were in place, the film was resumed, so that this second three-minute period of measurement was taken while Mrs. Reynolds dies and during the subsequent brief mourning scenes.

As soon as the film was over, the subjects were instructed to fill out a questionnaire in which they were asked to rate how tense or relaxed they felt before Mrs. Reynolds' death; how shocked they felt when they saw her head drop; how badly, how tense, and how upset they felt when they learned that she had just died; how tense they felt at that moment; how much they imagined themselves in Mrs. Reynolds' place (i.e., identification with her); how much they imagined themselves in the place of the student nurse (identification with the nurse); etc.

In addition, the subjects indicated how much and what kind of experience they had had working in hospitals prior to nursing school. These responses were sorted into four groups: no experience, experience up to eight months, more than eight months, and N.A. (not applicable). They were also asked whether they had been patients in hospitals, whether they had had any serious illnesses, and whether they had had any serious illnesses or deaths in their immediate families. Next they indicated their birth order and filled out the three items of the F-E scale.[3]

Results of the Film Study

Using palmar sweating as the indicator of empathetic arousal[4], all the other variables (including scores on the F-E scale, birth order, and questionnaire answers) were tested as predictors by means of the stepwise multiple linear regression analysis[5] (Efraymsen, 1960; Jensema, undated).

The results are shown in Table 4-1, Appendix D. It can be seen that palmar sweating related most strongly with the F-E scale. Although this relationship was not statistically significant, the relationship was positive and in the expected direction. On the other hand, there was a negative correlation between palmar sweating and subjects' ratings of how much they had imagined themselves in Mrs. Reynolds' position (identification with Mrs. Reynolds). The two variables—the F-E scale and degree of identification with Mrs. Reynolds—when considered jointly, controlled a statistically significant amount of variance. No other variables were significant predictors of palmar sweating either in isolation or in combination with other variables.

The negative relationship between the amount of palmar sweat registered and self-ratings of identification with Mrs. Reynolds was contrary to prediction. Furthermore, the identification self-ratings were significantly correlated (r = .28, p < .05) with scores on the F-E scale. In other words, the higher the score on the F-E scale, the more palmar sweat, but the less report of identification with Mrs. Reynolds.

To clarify these findings, an ANOVA of palmar sweat with three levels of scores on the F-E scale and three levels of the ratings of identification with Mrs. Reynolds was run. Both variables were independently and significantly (p < .05) related to palmar sweating. (See Table 4-2, Appendix B.) The fact that the F-E scale was significantly related to palmar sweat in this analysis, while only marginally significant in the regression analysis (p < .11) is due to the slight nonlinearity of the relationship between the two measures. The regression analysis tends to underestimate the strength of nonlinear relationships. While the interaction effect was only marginally significant (p < .10), an examination of the means for the various combinations of scale levels and rating levels revealed a curious pattern (Table 4-3, Appendix D). Subjects who were high on the F-E scale account for the bulk of the negative relationship between palmar sweat and self-ratings of identification with Mrs. Reynolds. Both the low and median level F-E scorers show tendencies toward curvilinearity in the relationship between the self-rating and palmar sweating. Thus, it appears that, if a subject was a high fantasizer, the more palmar sweat she registered, the less she reported imagining herself in the place of Mrs. Reynolds.

This peculiar pattern involves two processes that require explanation: first, the failure to report identification with Mrs. Reynolds by high fantasizers who showed a high amount of palmar sweat at the end of the film and second, the low degree of palmar sweat registered at the end of the film by high fantasizers who reported identification with Mrs. Reynolds.

Considering the first process, one plausible explanation would be that those students had identified *not* with Mrs. Reynolds, the patient, but with the young nursing student who was more similar to subjects in the study. Such an explanation was ruled out, however, because there was a positive, though nonsignificant correlation between the self-ratings of identification with the two film characters. Furthermore, identification with the student nurse was unrelated to palmar sweat (r = .079).

Turning to the second process, an equally plausible explanation for the lack of relationship between reported identification with Mrs. Reynolds and palmar sweat involves the timing of the physiological measurement. An analysis of the film's storyline indicates that most of the scenes in which Mrs. Reynolds suffered great pain occurred in the first half of the movie, long before the palmar sweat measurement. These scenes included the patient's discomfort in the hospital corridor, an emergency tracheotomy operation, Mrs. Reynolds' frantic effort to attract the attention of the nurses and attendants by clicking her false teeth, which were sitting on the table beside her, and other similar episodes. Due to the circumstances of the experiment, which had to be conducted within the time limits of a regular class period, only one palmar sweat measure could be fit in after the basal measurement at the beginning of the film. Because palmar sweat was recorded almost at the end of the movie, it could be argued that viewers who identified strongly with Mrs. Reynolds during the early scenes had no opportunity to demonstrate this in the physiological measurement.

To carry this argument a step further, perhaps these subjects who reported identification with Mrs. Reynolds, but showed a low level of palmar sweat at the end of the film had found their level of involvement with the patient in the early stages of the movie so anxiety-arousing and potentially painful that they tended to withdraw from the situation psychologically. Making their subsequent involvement purely intellectual would be a way of protecting themselves from painful empathy.

In light of data to be presented subsequently, such an explanation appears to be consistent with the results for both those subjects just described and for those high fantasizers who were not so highly involved with Mrs. Reynolds, and therefore would not have had to withdraw or intellectualize the situation. Thus, when the final measurement was taken, they would be expected to show a relatively high degree of palmar sweat on the occasion of the patient's death.

If this explanation of the reactions of the high fantasizers is correct, those high fantasizers, who were very highly involved in the film in general and who reported they felt tense before Mrs. Reynolds died, would also be expected to withdraw and intellectualize to protect themselves from a painful empathy experience. This possibility was explored by a three-way analysis of variance of palmar sweat using the same three levels of the F-E scale, two levels of the rating scale of identification with Mrs. Reynolds (instead of three),[6] plus two levels of the subjects' ratings of how tense they felt before Mrs. Reynolds died, as a measure of involvement prior to the patient's death.

The ANOVA produced a marginally significant F for the F-E scale. (See Table 4-4, Appendix D.) However, the interaction between identification and the F-E scale, which was only marginally significant in the previous analysis (Table 4-2, Appendix D), is now significant. This interaction results primarily from the high degree of palmar sweating by those who were high on the F-E scale, but identified little with Mrs. Reynolds. (See Table 4-5, Appendix D). In addition, this analysis shows a significant three-way interaction which reflects empathy being positively related to palmar sweat for all the identification and prior tension self-rating conditions except for subjects reporting high identification and high tension prior to Mrs. Reynolds' death. This interaction is striking because the F-E scale correlates .36 ($p < .05$) with self-ratings of tension prior to Mrs. Reynolds' death.

Thus, in general, it appears that those who responded physiologically to Mrs. Reynolds' death were those high on the F-E scale who were involved with the patient to some, but not an extreme, degree. The high empathizers, as reflected in palmar sweating, were either those who were generally low fantasizers who became involved with Mrs. Reynolds and who were tense when they did, or those who were high fantasizers but did not highly identify with Mrs. Reynolds. Those who otherwise might be expected to empathize strongly because they were high in fantasy and high in involvement in the situation were, in fact, relatively lower in empathy; note the score of only .26 for high fantasizers who were tense and identified with Mrs. Reynolds.

Although the amount of experience in hospitals prior to nursing school did not in itself correlate with palmar sweating, the possibility that experience in hospitals might have an interactive effect with the F-E scale was tested by means of an ANOVA. The degree of identification with Mrs. Reynolds was treated as a covariable in this ANOVA, because it had been found to have consistently significant effects on palmar sweat. There was a significant interaction, demonstrating that among higher fantasizers, those with a moderate amount of hospital experience palmar sweat more than those with a high amount and more than those with no hospital experience. (See Tables 4-6 and 4-7, Appendix D.) Those subjects with high experience and high F-E scores are not highly empathetic. In other words, high fantasy plus high experience in hospitals does not necessarily lead to empathizing. Those expected to empathize strongly because they were both high F-E scorers and experienced in the hospital may not have responded because of adaptation or because of defensive coping reactions (cf., Lazarus, 1966: Chapter 1). An alternative explanation of this finding may be selective mortality, that is, subjects who found they were prone to respond to other's suffering in a highly empathetic manner might have avoided continuing in a nursing career where their empathizing led to experiencing noxious emotional states.

Each of the separate questionnaire items concerning a person's degree of personal contact with illness did not relate to palmar sweating in the stepwise regression analysis. One possible reason for this might be that only an accumulation of personal experiences with illness (e.g., death in family plus own serious illness) would have an effect on empathy. Thus, an unweighted index was constructed, called Sum Contact with Illness, based on the sum of "yes" answers to the following items: being in hospital as patient, having had a serious illness, death in family, serious illness in family. Scores on this index were used in an ANOVA of palmar sweat, with the F-E scale as the other variable. Identification with Mrs. Reynolds was again used as the covariant. The Sum Contact with Illness was marginally significantly related to palmar sweat. (Table 4-8, Appendix D.) Those with the highest amount of contact with illness showed considerably more empathy, especially if they were high in fantasy. (Table 4-9, Appendix D.) In short, these data suggest that experience with illness leads a person to empathize more with people involved in illness. However, the effects of the F-E scale appear to be independent of this experience.

Although prior laboratory studies (see Chapter 1) have shown birth order to be a relevant variable in empathy, it was not found to relate to palmar sweating in the film study.

In summary, the main theme that runs through these results is that people who are high on fantasy may tend to avoid empathy when their reaction would lead them to experience very painful emotional states. This avoidance can take several forms. Those high fantasizers who, in watching the film, began by identifying to a high degree with Mrs. Reynolds, empathized less with her than those who began with less emotional investment. The first group could have psychologically or emotionally withdrawn from the situation that culminated in Mrs. Reynolds' death. High fantasizers who had considerable experience working in hospitals prior to entering nursing school also tended to empathize less than those who had little experience. Either those high fantasizers who empathized much with patients had temporarily dropped out of hospital work, or such high fantasizers had established defenses against high empathy. The latter would appear to be the more likely explanation, because it is improbable that those who had dropped out of hospital work because of painful empathetic experiences would later apply for nursing school.

It would appear then, from these results, that the relationship between fantasy scale scores, imaginative identification, recall of similar experiences, and empathetic responding is not as simple as initially hypothesized. The data suggest that for high fantasizers too much involvement from whatever source leads to various avoidance responses.

NOTES

1. The other empathy sub-scales that emerged in the factor analysis described in Chapter 2 were not used here because the F-E scale had received more validation and because the researchers were allowed only a very short time in the classroom to administer scales.

2. Our gratitude to the nursing students and their instructors for their cooperation: Judy Atwood, Susana Garner, Shirley Harlow, Barbara Innes, Maureen Niland, Jean Saxon, instructors.

3. At the end of the session the study was explained to the students and all questions were answered.

4. The palmar sweat data were analyzed by a procedure described in Chapter 1 (see Appendix B) in which the increase in sweating from the first to second measure is taken as a proportion of the baseline measure. Subjects who decrease in sweating are given a score of 0 increase, because there is no psychological reaction of palmar drying.

5. This analysis works in the following manner: At each step one variable is added to (or deleted from) the multiple regression equation. The variable that is added (or deleted) is the one that most reduces the error sum of squares. The reduction in error sum of squares is determined by picking the independent variable that has the highest partial correlation with the dependent variable partialed on the variables which have been previously added to the regression equation. That is, the F value of a variable added at any point in the analysis is determined solely by the unique variance controlled by that variable after the variance controlled by variables previously added to the regression analysis has been partialed from the dependent variable.

6. This change was made to insure adequate subject data for each of the 12 data cells. Because of the change, the results of this and the prior ANOVA cannot be expected to be entirely consistent.

Chapter 5

FANTASY AND HELPING IN HOSPITALS

Reporting research by Kenneth E. Mathews, Jr.
and Ezra Stotland

It is a popularly accepted but untested assumption that empathy is a personality trait that is necessary or at least desirable for members of the helping professions such as nursing. This belief may simply be the result of a principle of association well documented in social psychology (cf. Fritz Heider on proximity and causation): helpers are perceived to share the emotions of those they help, therefore, it is assumed empathy causes helping behavior.

The study by Mathews and Stotland of hospital experiences of nursing students to be reported in this chapter was based on

AUTHORS' NOTE: This research was supported by a grant from the National Science Foundation to Ezra Stotland. Our thanks to the administrators and staffs of the following Seattle hospitals: Doctors; Harborview; Swedish; St. Francis Cabrini; United States Veterans Administration Hospital.

a more specific and testable assumption: that a nurse who experiences negative affect because she empathizes with a patient can reduce that affect by making the patient more comfortable and by generally tending to the patient's needs.

There is empirical support for this rationale in the work of Aronfreed (see Chapter 1), who argued that the learned association between one's own and the other's pain leads to subsequent empathy with the other, although, as noted earlier, Aronfreed did not actually measure empathy. Mathews and Stotland went on to hypothesize that the association between one's own pain and that of the other is not the only road to empathy. Another is the individual's tendency to imagine the self in the other's position.

In the college term following the one in which the film study (Chapter 4) was conducted, the sophomore nursing students who had participated had their first exposure as students to actual hospital wards. In this setting, it was possible to test a prediction based on Aronfreed's theories, that highly empathetic nursing students would try harder to help patients and would therefore spend more time in the room of the patient assigned to them than would nurses low on the empathy dimension. It was assumed that these high empathizers would be more likely to imagine themselves in the place of the patient and would be reinforced by the reduction of their own emotional discomfort when they helped to reduce the patient's discomfort.

The hospital study was also designed to clarify the results of the film study described in Chapter 4. It had been predicted in the film study that nursing students who scored high on the F-E scale would imagine themselves more in the position of the patient whose death was depicted in the movie, would identify more with the patient, and would demonstrate more palmar sweat than low scorers when the patient's death was shown at the end of the movie. This prediction was based on laboratory studies of high F-E subjects (see Chapter 4). As noted, the results of the film study were not clear, because one group of high F-E subjects reported strong identification with the patient but demonstrated low levels of palmar sweat at the time of her death, whereas the other group of high F-E scorers did not report identification with the patient but showed a high degree of palmar sweat.

One possible explanation for the failure of the prediction in the film study was that those high fantasizers who identified strongly with the patient may have tended to intellectualize their involvement in order to avoid the pain aroused by their empathy, because when watching a film no helping response is possible (see for example Lazarus et al., 1962, cited in Chapter 1). Because the results of the film study had not been completely analyzed when the hospital study was begun, it was predicted that in the hospital situation persons who had showed a high degree of palmar sweating when watching the film, that is, high empathizers, would help patients more. It was also predicted that any variable which correlated with empathy, including scores on the F-E scale and amount of direct contact with illness, would also be correlated with the amount of help to patients as measured by the time spent in the patient's room.

The Hospital Setting

During the first week of the term the students met in regular classroom sessions for organization and orientation. The class was divided into 27 groups, each of which was to be sent to a different hospital under a different instructor. Mathews, the co-author, had not been present during the film study. He visited each class during the first week and requested the students' permission to be observed by him while on the hospital wards.[1] No information was given as to the purposes of the study; no mention was made of the connection between the film study and the hospital study.

During the eight-week period of the study the class met for one day per week at the hospitals. The wards were for the most part general medical or general surgical wards. No students were assigned to intensive treatment, pediatric, orthopedic surgery, isolation, or maternity wards. Although there were differences among the instructors, typically the students would arrive at the hospital at 7:30 a.m. for about an hour's instruction. Then, for approximately one and one-half hours, they would perform various duties for the patients to whom they were assigned, each being assigned to one patient. Their duties included making beds, hygienic care, taking temperatures, etc., but did not include distributing medicines. The instructor and nursing staff were available to the students for consultations during this time period.

Observations were made by the experimenter while standing at some central location in each of the wards. He did not enter the patients' rooms, but could observe the students directly while they were in the halls, at the nursing station, etc. He dressed in a lab coat so as to be viewed as part of the setting as much as possible.

On arriving in a ward, the observer would first attempt to identify each of the students by name. Next, he followed a procedure of observing each student for five minutes,[2] the order of observation being randomly determined. This usually permitted two to four observations of each student during the one day in which she was observed. Scheduling permitted only one day's observation of each subject. At least one group of students for each of the seven instructors who were teaching at one of the five hospitals was observed in the first four weeks and then at least one other group taught by the same instructor in the same hospital was observed in the last four weeks of the study.

The following categories of observation were used:

(1) Time in patient's room,

(2) Time in hallway,

(3) Time at nursing station,

(4) Time spent interacting with patients in hallway or at nursing station,

(5) Time spent interacting with other staff or students, and

(6) Numbers of interactions with others initiated.

The basic measure, then, was time spent in the patient's room. This measure was assumed to index helping behavior, because most of what a nurse is expected to do in the room is help the patient. A more direct measure of helping was impractical, because entering the room to observe the nurse-patient interaction would have raised ethical questions unless each pateint had given his or her consent.

While it was not possible to conduct a reliability check of the observation, it was felt that no large error was involved because the behavior observed was clearly delineated: the student was either in or out of a room.

The raw data were used to compute the following indices for each student:

(1) Percent of time in patient's room,

(2) Percent ot time in hallway (not including nurses' station),

(3) Percent of time at nurses' station,

(4) Percent of time in interaction with others,

(5) Percent of time (not including time in patient's room) in interaction with others,

(6) Number of interactions initiated,

(7) Percent of time in interaction with patients,

(8) Percent of time not in room and in interaction with patients,

(9) Number of interactions begun with patients,

(10) Percentage of time in interaction with others while in hallway, and

(11) Percentage of time in interaction with others at nursing station.

After the eight-week observation period was over, all subjects who had consented to be observed received memos explaining the study in full. They were then asked to mail back to the researchers filled-in questionnaires indicating their social security numbers, student numbers, and birth order, so that the data from the hospital study could be paired up with the data from the film study. In the latter study, the subjects had given these data, but had not given their names. After a follow-up mailing to the delinquent students, the percentage return was 87.8 of those who had been observed in the second study.

The planned overlap in samples of subjects in the Mrs. Reynolds film study and the hospital study[3] not only permitted an analysis of the relationships between empathy in the film study and helping in the hospital study, but also permitted the researchers to correlate hospital behavior with other questionnaire data from the film study. This data included time spent previously working in hospitals, experience as a patient or with relatives who were patients, and experience with death in the family.

Results of the Hospital Study

The data from the hospital observations were first subjected to a stepwise regression analysis, using the predictor variables employed in the regression analysis in the film study and three additional variables: amount of palmar sweating in the film study, hospital in which the observation was made, and week of observation.

In the regression analysis, palmar sweating, the index of empathy in the film study, showed no correlation at all with hospital behavior.

THE FANTASY SCALE

The F-E scale predicted ($F = 5.49$, $p < .05$) the percent of time in the patient's room, but the direction was opposite to that expected, that is, the higher the score on the F-E scale, the less time spent in the room. The time the high fantasizers spent out of the patient's room was used for interaction with patients and staff in the hallway, as shown by the relationships between F-E scale and the following:

Percent of time in hallways ($F = 4.05$, $p < .05$),

Percent of time while not in the patient's room spent interacting with patients ($F = 3.83$, $p < .05$),

Percent of time interacting with anyone in hall ($F = 8.43$, $p < .01$), and

Percent of time interacting with others ($F = 5.60$, $p < .05$).

Thus, the high F-E students avoided the patients in the rooms, but talked with patients and staff outside the rooms in the hallways. The meaning of these unexpected results will be analyzed below.

BIRTH ORDER

Although birth order did not relate to empathy in the film study, the first borns on the hospital ward showed some tendency also to stay out of the patients' rooms and to interact in the hallways and around the nursing station. Specifically, first borns spent less time in the patients' rooms ($F = 4.85$, $p < .05$), and more time at the nursing station ($F = 4.46$, $p < .05$); and they initiated more interactions with others ($F = 3.94$, $p < .05$).

PERIOD OF OBSERVATION

Not surprisingly, the students spent less time in the hallways and less time talking with others during the second four weeks than the first four of the term. This is shown by the relationships between the period of observation variable and the following:

Percent of time in hallways ($F = 6.51$, $p < .05$),

Percent of time interacting with others ($F = 7.93$, $p < .01$),

Percent of time not in patients' rooms spent interacting with others ($F = 8.48$, $p < .05$),

Number of interactions initiated ($F = 7.93$, $p < .05$), and

Percent of time in hall spent interacting with others ($F = 9.91$, $p < .01$).

OTHER PREDICTORS

Of the remaining predictor variables, only three were significantly related to more than one outcome variable in the regression analysis. Students who reported that they were more tense when they observed Mrs. Reynolds die also tended to spend more time at the nursing station ($F = 4.49$, $p < .05$); to spend a greater percentage of their time in interaction with others when they were not in patients' rooms (F = 6.16, p < .05); and to spend a greater percentage of their time in interaction with patients when not in patients' rooms (F = 5.60, p < .05).

Students who had had a death in their immediate family tended to interact more with others:

Percent of time interacting with others (F = 8.71, p < .01), and

Percent of time not in room interacting (F = 7.22, p < .01).

Students who had had some experience working in hospitals spent more time in interaction with patients:

Percent of time interacting with patients (F = 5.02, p < .05),

Percent of time interacting with all others as proportion of time not in patients' rooms (F = 5.37, p < .05), and

Number of interactions begun with patients (F = 14.45, p < .01).

Analyses of Outcome Variables

In addition to the stepwise regression analysis, the same analyses of variance, which produced significant results in the film study, were performed for each of the outcome variables in the hospital study. None of these ANOVAs produced any results not obtained in the regression analysis.

In order to better understand the negative relationship between the F-E scale and time spent in the patients' rooms, a number of additional ANOVAs were performed for the outcome variables, using as independent variables only those which had produced some significant results in previous analyses. Results of these ANOVAs for five of the outcome variables: percent of time in patient's room, percent of time in hallway, percent of time in nursing station, percent of time interacting with others, and percent of time interacting in hall, are shown in Table 5-1, Appendix D.

PERCENT OF TIME IN PATIENT'S ROOM

The most productive of the analyses of the percent of time subjects spent in the patients' rooms was one using the F-E scale, birth order, period of observation, and occurrence of family death as independent variables. As can be seen in Table 5.1, Appendix D, the significant effects of the F-E scale and birth order previously noted are also found in this analysis. Furthermore, there is a near-significant four-way interaction among the four independent variables. (Table 5-2, Appendix D, analyzes this and other interactions in more detail.) In trying to interpret the four-way interaction, a first useful step is to ignore the subjects who had had deaths in their families because the number of cell entries for these subjects were generally two or less. (See Table 5-2F, Appendix D for cell numbers.) Examining those subjects who had not had family deaths in Table 5-2A, Appendix D, the most striking difference occurs among first borns. During the first four weeks, the first borns high on the F-E scale spent only 31 percent of their time in the patients' rooms, while those lower on the scale spent around 70 percent of their time in the rooms. During the second four weeks, those lower on the scale tended to increase their percentage of time in the room slightly, while those high on the scale jumped 55 percentage points to 86 percent, the highest of any group.

Among the later borns, the picture is almost the opposite. Those high on the F-E scale tend to spend more time at first with the patients than those low, although both groups spend most of their time with them. In the second four weeks, the lows increase somewhat in time spent with the patient, just as is the case with first borns. However, the high fantasizers decrease in time spent, so that during the second four weeks they spend about 25 percent less time than the lows. In short, the first-born and later-born high empathizers appear to react in an opposite way to the hospital experience.

PERCENT OF TIME IN HALLWAYS

The shifts in behavior among the high fantasizers of different birth orders are also reflected in an analysis of the percent of

time spent in the hallways. This ANOVA shows the same significant four-way interaction we have just examined (F = 753,
p < .01). In Table 5-2B, Appendix D, we note the relatively high
percentage (32.6 percent) of time spent by high F-E first borns in
the hallways during the first four weeks, as contrasted with the
low of 5.6 percent in the second four weeks. Among later borns,
the corresponding percentages are 7.8 percent and 19.5 percent.
An ANOVA of the percent of time spent at the nursing station did
not yield a significant interaction. Nevertheless, on this variable
the first-born high fantasizers show a drop of 36 percent to 8.3
percent from the first to the second four-week period.

PERCENT OF TIME INTERACTING IN HALLS

In the four-way ANOVA performed on the percent of time not
in patients' rooms, which is spent talking with others in hallways,
an interaction between the F-E scale and birth order was found
(F = 3.532, p < .05). This appears to reflect the fact that among
first borns, high fantasizers interact more than lows, while the
tendency does not generally occur among later borns. Thus, the
tendency of the F-E scale to make sharper predictions among first
borns is manifest in this analysis also.

FAMILY DEATH, PERIOD OF OBSERVATION,
AND BIRTH ORDER

In the first ANOVA discussed, that of the percentage of time
spent in the patients' rooms (Table 5-1, Appendix D), there were
two other significant interactions. The first was between period
of observation and family death. This appears to reflect the
tendency for those who had experienced family deaths to spend
about the same percentage of time in the rooms as those who had
not had a death during the first four weeks, while during the
second four-week period, those who had not experienced family
deaths tended to rise in time spent in the rooms and those who
had had deaths tended to withdraw. The other significant interaction, that between birth order, week of observation, and death
in the family, appears to reflect the fact that the tendencies just

described occur more strongly among the first borns than the later borns. If we look at the data in Table 5-1, we see that there is an indirect reflection of this tendency in the significant interaction between birth order, family death, and period of observation in the ANOVA of percent of time spent in the hall ($F = 7.608$, $p < .01$), and also by the same interaction in the percent of time in hall spent in interacting ($F = 4.886$, $p < .05$). The first borns who have had deaths in their families tend to maintain a higher level of interaction than those who have not had deaths, during both the first four and final four weeks. On the other hand, the later borns show this difference between death and no death only during the first four weeks. They drop in their interactions with others during the final four weeks.

Patterns of Avoiding Empathy

A common theme appears in the results of the hospital and film studies. The theme is that people who are high in fantasy tend to avoid involvement in situations in which their empathy would lead them to experience very painful emotional states. In the film study, this avoidance can only be inferred from the lack of response to the palmar sweating measure evidenced by those high fantasizers who said they identified most strongly with Mrs. Reynolds. In the hospital study, nursing students with high F-E scores initially spent significantly less time than other students in the patients' rooms and interacted more with patients and others in the hallways. These tendencies were particularly marked for firstborn students.

The prediction, based on Aronfreed's studies, that those who experienced negative affect would reduce this painful emotion by making the patient more comfortable was not supported, if we confine our observations to the first four-week period of the study. Instead of helping patients, subjects seem to have avoided the painful empathetic experience by staying out of the room, and to have sought support from staff nurses and other hospital personnel. Why was the prediction not confirmed? One possibility is that no simple response, such as the one learned by

Aronfreed's child subjects (Aronfreed, 1968) was available to turn off the patient's pain and thus reduce the nursing student's anxiety. Although staying out of the patient's room could cut down on painful empathy, it could have led to anxiety about the tendency to avoid the patient. Both of these negative emotions may be what led these high fantasizers to spend time talking with others in the hall.

These patterns of avoidance of the high empathy-arousing situation and the seeking of supportive relationships with others appear to have occurred more among first borns than among later borns. At first the high fantasy first borns seem to seek support from the staff nurses and other hospital personnel. This pattern of first borns seeking dependency relationships with others as a way of handling anxiety has been found in a number of studies (e.g., Schachter, 1959). In fact, the first borns in general, regardless of their level of fantasy, tended to stay out of the patients' rooms to spend more time at the nursing station, and to interact more with others. However, for the high fantasizers, this turning to others for support appears to have had a long range positive effect: in the second four weeks they returned to the patients' rooms to spend over 85 percent of their time in them. When they had received some sort of reassurance or good practical advice on how to relate to patients, they may have had less need to avoid the high empathy situation. We can only speculate as to whether they simply empathized less on their return to the rooms, or whether they were able to cope better with their emotions, or with the patients' problems. If the explanation is an increase in ability to cope with the patients' problems, then Aronfreed's (1968) reasoning is vindicated, because he points out that the child needs to learn what to do in order to reduce the other's pain.

This tendency of first borns to seek support in the face of anxiety-arousing situations also probably underlies the tendency found for first borns who have had death in their families to spend less time in the patients' rooms in the latter four weeks. In all probability, they encountered some deaths or near deaths among patients during the first four weeks, which re-aroused the negative emotions associated with their own experiences with death. They then withdrew from the rooms to spend more time out in the hall, interacting with others.

The results for the later borns were not nearly so suggestive as for the first borns. In some analyses they not only showed no results like those of the first borns, they sometimes showed opposite effects. Some of the differences between first borns and later borns may be due to differences in the amount of practical experience gained in the early part of the study. Since later born, high F-E subjects spent much more time (about 70 percent) with patients during the first four weeks, they had an opportunity to become more practical, efficient, and fast in performing their duties and comforting the patients. As they became more practiced, they may have needed less time with the patients to render essentially the same services.

A puzzle remains as to why palmar sweating in the film study did not relate to behavior in the hospital study. This puzzle becomes greater when one sees that the F-E scale predicts both palmar sweating and behavior in the hospital. It may be that palmar sweating, as one of several different possible expressions of emotion, was too limited a reaction to predict gross behavior some months later. It may be that the F-E scale taps a complex of tendencies which are related to palmar sweating and gross behavior, but not so highly as to necessitate the latter being related to each other.

The question raised at the beginning of this chapter, then, whether or not empathy is a necessary or desirable trait in the helping professions, was not resolved in this study. It is clear that empathy as measured by the F-E scale interacts with both birth order and a number of other situational variables, so as to make predictions in specific cases difficult. In the next chapter, further studies of the relationship between empathy and helping will be described.

NOTES

1. Approximately 85 percent of the students present at that time complied with this request. Five of the 127 subjects in the film study did not continue the second term.

2. Because the student nurses were not usually in each room for more than five minutes, the length of time was considered reasonable.

3. Behavioral data in the hospital setting was analyzed only for subjects who met all the following criteria: (a) participated in the Mrs. Reynolds film study, (b) gave prior permission for the hospital observations, (c) were present at the hospital and working on the ward on the one day that observations were made on subjects' particular instructional group (frequently a subject would be present but working with her assigned patient in another portion of the hospital), and (d) answered the questionnaire requesting information which would allow matching the film study data with behavioral data. Although compliance was better than 85 percent with requests (b) and (d) above, the cumulative effect of both noncompliance and absence at each stage resulted in a final subject total of approximately 60 percent of the subjects in the film study.

Chapter 6

EMPATHY AND HELPING

Reporting research by Kenneth E. Mathews, Jr.,
Larry K. Davis, Robert O. Hansson, Warren H. Jones,
and Joy Hammersla

A middle-aged man collapses on a subway train . . . a woman's purse is snatched and she is pushed down a flight of stairs . . . a motorist with a flat tire tries to flag down a car along a busy highway. Eventually someone stops and offers help, while others pass by. Is it empathy that motivates the Good Samaritans?

During the past decade, psychologists have researched the field of altruistic, pro-social behavior in the laboratory and in many imaginatively designed field experiments (Bleda, 1976). In the explanations they have come up with, empathy typically plays a part. One research paradigm for studying spontaneous helping behavior has been termed the "empathetic arousal model" (Piliavin et al., 1969):

Observation of an emergency creates an emotional arousal in the bystander. It will be differentially interpreted in different situations (Schachter 1964) as fear, disgust, sympathy, etc. . . . This state of arousal is higher (a) *the more one can empathize with the victim* [emphasis added] . . . (b) the closer one is to the emergency, and (c) the longer the state of emergency continues without the intervention of a helper. It can be reduced by (a) helping directly (b) going to get help (c) leaving the scene . . . (d) rejecting the victim as undeserving.

One of the unanswered questions that this model raises is the structure of the relationship between aroused empathy and helping or not helping. Further, while empathy is recognized as a variable of importance in theories of this type, research is rare in which empathy is clearly defined and independently recorded and measured.

One theory of altruistic behavior that attempts to define empathy as a personality variable and to measure its correlates is that of Schwartz (1968, 1970, 1973). The definition that Schwartz supplies for the key trait "awareness of consequences" (AC) is: "a relatively stable individual tendency to think about situations in terms of their consequences for the welfare of others" (Schwartz, 1973). While the term "think" has a cognitive flavor, Schwartz goes on to state that AC, which is measured by a projective test for the purposes of his research, involves "sharing the subjective experience of those whose welfare one may affect" (Schwartz, 1968). This latter is very close to the definition of empathy adopted here from Stotland. In addition, AC is conceived to involve the two processes that Stotland has called "simple" and "contrast" empathy, because according to Schwartz this variable "need not represent favorable orientation to the object," but can include a sadistic reaction. Schwartz's research on AC as an individual difference variable demonstrated significant correlations between high AC scores and peer ratings of altruistic dispositions including considerateness, helpfulness, and reliability.

Closeness to the emergency or the victim, another variable in the "empathetic arousal" model, has been varied in a number of studies. Proximity has been shown to be a strong inhibitor of aggressive behavior, particularly where there is feedback from the victim (Milgram, 1965; Buss, 1966a; Buss, 1966b; Tilker, 1970). In the paradigm developed by Milgram where subjects are ordered to give electric shocks in the "teacher" role, the decreased aggression with increased proximity to the victim could well result from the empathetic arousal that Schwartz has called "awareness of the consequences of one's own behavior for others." In two experiments using the Milgram paradigm, Barton (1971a and b) has shown that proximity reduced both the shock level and duration of shocks applied. Even in cases where the aggressor had been previously angered or insulted by the victim, aggression by the male college students Baron studied decreased substantially as magnitude of pain cues increased.

There is also evidence that persons who are high in empathy are. more sensitive than others to the proximity of a victim. Mehrabian and Epstein (1972) administered a 33-item self-report questionnaire designed to measure emotional empathy to male and female college students. A week later, subjects participated in an electric shock session modeled after Baron (1971a) with two levels of proximity to the victim, but without oral feedback. Baron's overall results were not replicated, but a significant interaction between empathy and immediacy indicated that those subjects scoring high on empathy administered less shock to persons in the same room with them than to those in an adjoining room.

Both Stotland et al. (see Chapter 1) and Schwartz have emphasized the importance of observational set on the prospective empathizer. In a replication of Lerner's "Just World" study of the derogation of a victim (Lerner and Simmons, 1966), Aderman, Brehm, and Katz (1974) found that while Lerner's instructions to his subjects to "watch" the behavior of a victimized individual in a tape-recorded sequence resulted in downgrading the victim, instructions based on Stotland et al. to "imagine themselves" in the other's situation led subjects to rate the victim as more attractive than the self. Subjects run individually also rated the victim higher than those run in groups as in the Lerner experiment. In the Aderman et al. study, as in the "Mrs. Reynolds" film study reported in Chapter 4, no opportunity was given to demonstrate overt helping behavior.

The studies of student nurses by Stotland and Mathews described in Chapters 4 and 5 were designed to examine the relationship between the variables of empathy and helping, but the results raised as many questions as they answered. For example, in Chapter 5 the researchers had expected that nurses who empathized more would establish closer contacts with patients and spend more time in the patients' rooms. The prediction of positive linear relationship between empathy and helping was based partially on the work of Aronfreed and Paskal (Aronfreed, 1968) described in Chapter 1. However, the data in the nursing study did not support this approach, because the higher the individual's score on the F-E scale, the less time this person spent with patients during the initial hospital observation period.

The Seattle Crisis Clinic, a voluntary organization which provides 24-hour telephone help for persons in emotional crisis, was the setting for a study designed by Mathews (unpublished) to clarify the results of the hospital study. Mathews investigated the relationship between scores on the F-E test and the helping behavior of volunteer workers in the clinic. In addition to Aronfreed's model, Mathews tested the fit of his data to two additional theories about the relationship between empathy and helping: (a) an escape-reinforcement theory which would assume a linear negative relationship between empathy and helping, and (b) an "empathy-situation interaction" model, based on the assumption that as a potential helper's level of emotional arousal increases, the probability of helping another individual at first increases, reaches a peak, and then begins to decrease.

While the S-R escape-reinforcement explanation seemed to fit the data in the hospital study, it failed to account for the results of the film study, particularly the unexpected negative relationship between identification with the patient in the film and degree of palmar sweating among subjects who were high fantasizers.

Subjects in Mathews study were 43 nonprofessional part-time telephone answerers at the Crisis Clinic. These persons were required to deal with and report two types of calls: crisis calls, defined as those that "pose an immediate physical or psychological threat to the person seeking assistance,"[1] and chronic calls, or those that presented either a nonserious or a recurring problem, based on the case files maintained in the clinic. Regulations of the clinic required that every effort be made to complete chronic calls in five minutes or less.

For the purpose of the study, Mathews defined helping behavior operationally as time on the phone interacting with distressed callers. It was assumed that on the whole the probability of making a helping response was constant for any given unit of time. Therefore, as the total time interacting increased, it was assumed that the total amount of help given to another also increased.

Data obtained from the subjects included their F-E scores, birth order, sex, age, and length of time working at the Crisis Clinic. Subjects, all of whom were volunteers, constituted 78 percent of the 55 nonprofessional telephone answerers employed at the clinic. They included two distinct groups, students from the college work-study program and older volunteer workers.

Crisis Clinic procedure required telephone workers to record data on each call answered including the date, time received, time terminated (if more than five minutes in length), name of caller, name of answerer, type of call, and comments. Records for the five-month period from September 1, 1971, to January 31, 1972, were inspected to obtain the mean amount of time spent talking to crisis callers and the mean amount of time talking to chronic callers for each of the 43 subjects. Because of the variability of types and seriousness of presenting problems for both crisis and chronic calls, it was decided to analyze data only from those subjects who had answered some minimal number of each of these two types of calls. Thus, 34 (of the 43 original subjects) persons who had answered at least five crisis calls during the first and second halves of the five-month period were selected as the main sample. A more stringent criterion of having answered at least two chronic calls in both halves of the study produced another sample of 17 individuals who had answered, in addition, at least 12 crisis calls during each of the two periods.

It was assumed that a positive relationship between empathy scores and time spent on the telephone would support Aronfreed's theory, a negative relationship would support the S-R escape theory, while the situation-interaction theory would require a negative relationship between telephone time and empathy on crisis calls plus a nonsignificant or curvilinear relationship on chronic calls where the empathy-arousal cues would be fewer. It was further predicted that birth order would interact with empathy to moderate the predicted effects.

The predictions were tested by stepwise regression analysis for linear effects and by eta coefficients and analyses of variance for possible curvilinear effects. In the regression program, F-E score, birth order, sex, age, months of experience, and type of subject (volunteer or work-study program) were used as predictor variables for the mean time spent interacting on crisis and chronic calls. No significant empathy results were obtained in the regression analysis.

Some data of interest in relating F-E scores to helping behavior was developed in a two-way ANOVA involving F-E scores and birth order effects on time interacting on the phone. Fantasy-empathy scores were split into three levels and separate analyses were run for crisis and chronic calls. For the larger sample (N = 32), high F-E scorers were shown to spend significantly more time on the phone than low scorers for crisis calls. There was no significant effect for chronic calls, possibly due to the ceiling effect created by the five-minute limitation. A similar analysis was run for the sample of 17 subjects for whom more chronic calls were available. Again, there was no significant result for the chronic calls, but on crisis calls high fantasizers talked-significantly longer. In this sample, however, the birth order interaction was significant, and it was shown that the results for interaction time on the phone were due to high fantasizers who were later borns. First and only high F-Es spent significantly less time than later borns on the phone. This confirms the results in the hospital study where first and only subjects spent significantly less time in the patients' rooms than did later borns, but the explanation here is less clear because we have no data in regard to first borns seeking advice and reassurance by interacting with others. Certainly, this may have happened.

While Mathews' findings on birth order interactions give a good indication that empathy was being measured in his Crisis Clinic study, the results were not clear-cut, particularly because none of the variables in his regression equation predicted helping behavior as defined in the study.

How anxiety-arousing were the crisis calls answered by the volunteers studied by Mathews? In order to test the situation-interaction model in particular, it is necessary to provide different levels of arousal cues. It was not possible to simply test the difference between time spent on chronic and crisis calls, because chronic calls were treated differently than crisis calls due to the instructions given to limit them to five minutes. It would seem from the description given (see Note 1) that the crisis calls were too variable among and within themselves to provide any reliable effects.

This interpretation is strengthened by the results of another study carried out in a similar population by Davis, Hansson, and Jones (1975) at the Tulsa Hotline. Tulsa's Hotline Crisis Intervention Service, like the Seattle Crisis Clinic, provides a 24-hour telephone counseling service and is staffed by volunteer counselors. The hotline researchers limited their analysis to "suicide" calls, that is, calls during which the person on the line threatened to take his own life.[2]

Subjects in the Tulsa study were 29 volunteers (13 male, 16 female) ranging in age from 19 to 60 years. The subjects were pretested on the Machiavellianism V scale (Christie and Geis, 1970), as well as on the F-E scale, and their birth order was recorded. They were not told what follow-up procedures would be undertaken. All calls received by the 29 volunteers during the next three months were reviewed. A record of every call is made at the agency, which includes name of answerer, type of call, and exact length of time spent on the phone. From these records the average length of each subject's suicide calls during the three-month period was calculated.

The data were analyzed by correlating the mean length of each volunteer's suicide calls with his empathy score and his score on

Machiavellianism. The number of suicide calls a volunteer received during the three-month period ranged from 2 to 12. The mean length of all suicide calls was 59.7 minutes. A significant correlation was obtained between empathy and mean length of suicide calls (r = —.34, p < .05), indicating that high scorers on the F-E scale spent less time on the telephone with potential suicides. Machiavellianism was not significantly related to mean length of suicide calls (r = .15, N.S). In this sample, the correlation between the F-E scale and the Mach V scale, while negative, was nonsignificant (r = —.226). Thus the data in this study are consistent with the hospital study. However, there were no birth order effects or interactions.

Empathy and Bystander Helping

In the situation-interaction model of the relationship between empathy and helping described earlier, the prediction was made that persons scoring high on the F-E scale would be more likely to help another person in a situation of moderate stress than in situations producing high anxiety such as the hospital and the answering of a suicide call. It was not possible for Mathews to give this hypothesis an effective test, due to the time limit placed on chronic calls in the Seattle Crisis Clinic.

A test of this hypothesis was therefore arranged by Joy Hammersla (1974) at the University of Washington as part of a larger study of the effects of participation in a laboratory-intervention experiment on subsequent attitudes and on helping behavior in a naturalistic setting. The stimulus in Hammersla's study was designed to induce moderate intensities of empathic arousal, and the prediction was that high fantasizers would be more likely to help than to avoid the "victim" of an arranged incident, especially because the helping response was immediately available, was easily within the capability of all subjects, and was not costly.

Subjects in Hammersla's study were female college freshmen enrolled in a large introductory course in psychology, who were given bonus points for their participation. Out of a total of 150 subjects who took part in the larger study, 78 participated in the phase that tested spontaneous helping behavior. All subjects had taken the F-E scale, as well as the Mehrabian-Epstein test of emotional empathy (Mehrabian and Epstein, 1972) in the classroom, and had indicated their birth orders.

In the portion of the study of interest here, subjects, accompanied by a confederate of the experimenter, crossed the campus from one building to another when, on a parking lot about ten feet away from them, a girl (a trained model) dropped a bag of books and papers and burst into tears. In all cases, the confederate looked but "maintained an impassive composure." In the meantime the confederate was rating the subject on the degree to which she responded, based on the time spent helping the other girl. A rating of 0 was given for no help at all, a 1 if subject spoke to the other, 2 if she picked up some of the books and papers, and 3 if she continued to help until the other girl left in her car with her books and papers.

Scores on neither the F-E scale nor the Mehrabian-Epstein scale were significantly correlated with helping behavior in the overall data analysis. Birth order was also unrelated to helping: 54 percent of the first born and 50 percent of the later borns helped. However, when the F-E scores of first and later borns were correlated separately with the dependent variable of helping, a familiar pattern of interaction emerged. In this case it was the first born, high F-E scorers who helped. There was a significant point-biserial correlation of .46 ($p < .05$) between F-E scores and helping for the first borns (N = 24), whereas there was no relationship at all for the 54 later borns (r = .01).

As pointed out above, some differences between Hammersla's manipulation and the hospital and Crisis Clinic-Hotline studies were that a minimum of anxiety is likely to have been aroused in the helping manipulation, and that here the subjects were not in a position where failure to help would be seen as failing to do their job. In an effort to illuminate subjects' various perceptions of the situation, a postexperimental questionnaire was administered. One (later born) subject made a suggestive comment: "I . . . felt that if it was me, I'd rather have people go on than stop, so I went on." Applying Stotland's theory of social schemas, such a comment suggests that in some later borns this situation may have aroused an equal-status-peer oriented schema, whereas in the first borns the schema aroused may have been on the dominance-dependency dimension. Helping a distraught but not endangered girl might be seen as a parent-child type response, characteristic of first borns.

Pattern of Results

The pattern of relationships among fantasy, empathy, birth order, and helping behavior that emerges from these varied studies in natural settings is complex. While in none of the studies do we have clear-cut support for Mathew's situation-interaction model, there is some data that indicates it may be predictive, at least for first borns. Certainly none of the studies substantiates an overall direct linear relationship between empathy and helping behavior.

In the hospital studies, where a number of variables including contact with illness and death, high F-E scores, and birth order all interacted, there appeared to be some point at which emotional arousal led to avoidance of involvement both with characters in a film and with hospital patients. In the Crisis Clinic and on the Hotline again, high situational demands plus high empathic arousal tended to decrease helping behavior for first borns. In the situation of the bystander study, birth order was also the best positive predictor of helping behavior for those high on the F-E scale. To decipher the pattern emerging from these various studies will probably require a return to the laboratory where better control can be exercised over the situational variables.

NOTES

1. Nason (1970) randomly selected files on 200 crisis calls recorded at the Seattle clinic for detailed study and found that complaints of feeling lonely, depressed, fearful, or inadequate constituted 37 percent; marital conflict 28 percent; threats of suicide 19 percent; psychiatric symptoms such as hallucinations, anxiety attacks, and delusions, 15 percent; financial and employment problems, 12 percent; and fear of violence in oneself or others, 11 percent. (Thirty percent included more than one type of complaint.)

2. Statistics for the January-June 1975 period indicate that of a total of 7,870 calls received, 2.1 percent were classified as suicide calls.

Chapter 7

EMPATHY AS A PERSONALITY CONSTRUCT

Reporting research by Robert O. Hansson,
Kenneth E. Mathews, Jr., and Mildred Disbrow

Something more than situational factors must account for differences in empathy. The empathetic variable extends over a
spectrum which ranges from the deep empathies of a Shakespeare
to the fixed and self-centered perspectives of a schizophrenic
personality.

—Katz (1963: 57-58)

Is there an empathetic personality? Katz was one of many to
call attention to individual differences in empathetic responding,

AUTHORS' NOTE: A portion of the data reported in this chapter was collected in collaboration with D. M. Nebeker, in connection with another project supported by Contract
N00014-67-A-0103-0012, Office of Naval Research, Department of the Navy, and Contract N00014-67-A-0103-0013, Advanced Research Projects Agency, Office of Naval
Research (Fred E. Fiedler, Principal Investigator). Data reported in study 2 were gathered in collaboration with K. Mathews.

and with the development of the F-E scale, a tool is available to differentiate between individuals on this variable. Researchers have begun to explore the question of what other personality characteristics, if any, empathetic responders have in common.

In the first validation studies of the various empathy scales (Chapter 2), it was shown that in a sample of 516 college underclassmen, fantasy scores were unrelated to a number of standard personality scales developed by I. Sarason (1958). The one exception was a small but significant positive correlation (r = .19) with Sarason's "anxiety when hostile" scale. The studies reported in this chapter again failed to find significant correlations between F-E and a number of widely used personality scales, giving further indication that empathy is an independent behavior tendency. This interpretation is strengthened by the fact that in a college student population similar to that tested on Sarason's scales, a significant positive correlation of .47 was found by Hammersla (1974) between the three-item F-E scale and a new 33-item self-report questionnaire on emotional empathy developed by Mehrabian and Epstein (1972).

Empathy and Interpersonal Perception

A promising line of inquiry deals with cognitive characteristics which might facilitate or inhibit empathetic responding, and leads to the study of interpersonal perceptions. Individuals who score high on the F-E scale have been shown to tend, more than others, to imagine themselves in the position of another person. Findings reported in this chapter indicate that high fantasizers, perhaps as a result of such identifications, differ from other people in their perceptions of human nature in general and in their evaluations of and attraction to others whose characteristics or attitudes are dissimilar to their own.

One way of characterizing empathetic responding is to see it as an emotional investment in the feelings and problems of other people. Robert Hansson reasoned that having a negative view of people in general would be inconsistent with such an investment, and he gave a series of questionnaires to test the hypothesis that an individual's score on the F-E scale would be positively related to his evaluations of human nature in general.

Subjects were 62 undergraduate students at the University of Washington, comprising three sections of an introductory social psychology course. They completed the questionnaires as a group in their classrooms. In addition to the F-E scale, the main instrument was Wrightsman's "philosophies of human nature" scale (Wrightsman, 1964; 1972). The six subscales or dimensions indexed by Wrightsman are (1) trustworthiness, (2) strength of will and rationality, (3) altruism, (4) independence, (5) complexity and understandability, and (6) variability. Scores are also compiled on favorability of human nature (sum of the first four scales), and the multiplexity of human nature (sum of the last two scales). It was predicted that persons scoring high on the F-E scale would have more positive views of human nature than low scorers. The Mach IV scale (Christie and Geis, 1970) was also included in this study, because those high on Machiavellianism are considered to have a negative view of human nature.

All eight correlations between the F-E scale and the dimensions of Wrightsman's scale were positive, and three of them reached statistical significance. (See Table 7-1, Appendix D.) Contrary to the prediction, scores on the Mach IV scale were unrelated to scores on the F-E scale.[1]

Results of Hansson's study lend some support to his prediction that high empathy persons regard others positively, although only the dimension of altruism yielded a significant correlation. More interesting is the finding that these high fantasizers perceive other people as more variable and dissimilar to each other and human nature as more multiplex than do low scorers. It seems logical that persons who make a practice of identifying with others should learn to make finer discriminations among people than those who do not. (Birth order data were not used in this study.)

Empathy and Negative Stereotypes

Persons who have learned to perceive others as variable and multiplex should be less likely to make negative generalizations about people of another race, class, or nationality. Another Hansson study tested this willingness to make negative generalizations or to stereotype others, using a sample of 21 white undergraduates, constituting all of the Caucasians in an introductory psychology course at the University of Washington. All subjects had previously taken the F-E scale, and they participated as a group in their classroom and received course credit. The instrument was a "disguised structure" test in which subjects were asked to make statistical estimates about characteristics of children with one black and one white parent, including predicting such variables as intelligence, drug usage, and college attendance. The dependent variable was the willingness to make negative evaluations.

Hansson's prediction that high empathizers would be less willing to ascribe negative characteristics to persons racially dissimilar to themselves was confirmed.

Based on the findings in earlier studies by Stotland (see Chapter 1) that experimentally induced empathy interacted with birth order, Hansson also analyzed birth order data in this study. As the theory would predict, those high F-Es who were least willing to stereotype persons of a dissimilar race tended to be first borns, and this group accounted for most of the relationship between the F-E scale and the predictions about the black children. Again, Hansson's data confirm the interaction of birth order and empathy and lend support to the validity of the F-E scale.

Empathy and Interpersonal Attraction

There is some evidence, then, that persons high on empathy have learned to make finer discriminations among people. Do these high empathizers differ from others in the way they choose their friends? Among the factors that have been shown to influence interpersonal attraction are physical proximity (Festinger et al., 1950), familiarity (Zajonc, 1968; Harrison, 1969), physical appearance (Walster et al., 1966), and perceived similarity (Byrne, 1971), to cite only a few studies.

A study by Kenneth E. Mathews, Jr. focused on the relation-ship between empathy as measured by the F-E scale and the rewarding effects of similarity of attitudes and beliefs on the variable of interpersonal attraction. The hypothesis, based on Byrne's findings (Byrne, 1969; 1971) that manipulating the degree of belief congruence affects interpersonal attraction, was that high fantasizers would be more sensitive to such manipulated similarities and differences in beliefs than would low F-E scorers. Thus, it was predicted that highs would be more likely than lows to be attracted to others on the basis of belief congruence. A second prediction, based on the studies of Stotland et al. (see Chapter 1), was that birth order would interact with empathy in the attraction ratings of dissimilar others.

Subjects in the Mathews study were 45 undergraduates en-rolled in an introductory social psychology class at the University of Washington. They were tested in their classroom during two regular class sessions and received bonus points toward their grades. In the first session subjects filled out the F-E scale, the Marlowe-Crowne social desirability scale (1961), Rotter's I-E scale (1966), and Watson & Friend's "fear of negative evaluation" scale (1969) which is also known as a "test of social anxiety." They indicated their birth order and filled out a second booklet recording their attitudes on 12 topics (items obtained from Byrne, 1966).

At a second session two weeks later in a procedure similar to that described by Byrne (1966), subjects were each given two booklets specially constructed for each person based on their answers to the attitude scales taken earlier. One booklet described a person who was in 75 percent disagreement with the subjects and the other, a person in 75 percent agreement. Each booklet was followed by Byrne's interpersonal judgment scale (IJ). Order of presentation of the two booklets was counterbalanced. Subjects were instructed to read the responses that were checked in each booklet, attempt to form some impression of what kind of person would have responded in such a manner, and to rate that person on the IJ scale.

Three dependent variables were obtained from the IJ scales: first, the rating of the similar other; second, the rating of the dissimilar other; and third, the difference between the two ratings. The IJ scale was scored in such a way that a high score indicated a high level of attraction.

Results of the study indicated that high empathizers were in general more sensitive to differences in attitudes and beliefs than to similarities (see Table 7-2, Appendix D). As predicted, there was a significant ($p < .05$) correlation ($r = .301$) between empathy and the difference between the ratings of the similar and dissimilar other. This significant finding was due to a negative correlation ($r = .275$, $p < .05$) between empathy and the rating of the dissimilar other, indicating that the more empathetic the subject, the lower the evaluation of the dissimilar other. The correlation between F-E and evaluation of the similar other did not reach significance.

As in previous studies, high scores on fantasy failed to correlate significantly with either birth order or the standard personality measures (see Table 7-3, Appendix D).

To test the predicted interaction between empathy and birth order for the evaluation of the dissimilar other, an analysis of variance was performed, using a least squares model. Fantasy-empathy scale scores were divided into three levels and birth order into two levels. Although the data tended in the right direction, the combination of empathy scale scores into the three groups reduced the significance of the relationship between empathy and the evaluations, resulting in marginal significance for the main effect of empathy and the interaction between empathy and birth order (see Table 7-4, Appendix D).

In order to obtain a more sensitive test of the hypothesized difference between birth orders, correlations were separately computed for first-and-only and for later-born subjects (see Table 7-5, Appendix D). As in Hansson's study, the results demonstrated that the significant negative correlations between empathy and evaluation of dissimilar others among the later-born subjects accounted for the overall rejection of the dissimilar other by high empathizers.

The finding that the negative correlation between empathy and the attraction to a dissimilar other is significantly greater for later borns than for first-and-onlies provides additional support for the assertion that the F-E scale is in fact measuring empathy.

Results of the Hansson and Mathews studies lend some insight into the cognitive styles of the highly empathetic person. Skills developed in feeling the emotions of others lead to more accuracy in discriminating differences between people. Whether the highly empathetic person will be less attracted than the low empathizer to persons seen as dissimilar to the self or whether, on the other hand, this high empathizer will be less likely than the low scorer to downgrade and stereotype persons and groups seen as dissimilar will depend on other individual difference variables such as birth order.

So far, studies recounted in this chapter have focussed on characteristics of persons who are high scorers on the F-E scale. What of the low empathizer? A recent research project at the University of Washington represents a first step in exploration of the personality correlates of low scorers on the empathy scale.

Empathy and Child Abuse

Sometimes the change of focus that occurs with attempts at clinical application of research findings yields new data and raises new questions. The campaign against child abuse and neglect has recently led to the passage of laws in all 50 states making reporting of child abuse cases mandatory. This made possible the accumulation of empirical data on the characteristics of parents and guardians who abuse or neglect children. People began to ask: How can we identify potential child abusers? The research of Dr. Mildred Disbrow at the University of Washington School of Nursing seeks to answer this question. In her search for possible personality correlates of child abuse and neglect, her focus is on individuals who would be expected to score low on the empathy scale.

Planned as a longitudinal study of known child abusers and neglectors, Dr. Disbrow's research is aimed at prevention via the early identification of individuals with potential for child abuse in stressful situations. The first phase of the study, the development of a predictive test battery, began in 1974 and was completed in March 1977 (Disbrow et al., 1977). Subjects were 55 abusive and neglective families (including both single parents and couples) who volunteered for the study after referral by the Child Protective Service of the Washington State Department of Social and Health Services. They were matched to a control sample of 54 families on the basis of the mother's age, education, race, and marital status, and the ages of the children, which ranged from infancy to two and one-half. The entire sample included 169 individuals (109 females and 60 males).

In constructing her predictors of child abuse, Dr. Disbrow used home interviews with taped interactions of parents and children, attitude scales, and personality tests. The personality measures included all five of the empathy scales designed by Stotland and Sherman (see Chapter 2) and the Mach IV scale (Christie and Geis, 1970). Finally, in an effort to chart subjects' reactions to stress, their physiological responses were measured while they watched a film, a procedure rather similar to the manipulation in the Mrs. Reynolds study described in Chapter 3. The film in this case was designed for the study, and it represented parents interacting with their children in situations that were alternatively pleasant or stressful, with intervals of neutral music.

Preliminary results of research on 22 families (12 matched couples and 10 matched single parents) were analyzed in a correlational matrix, using Kendall's Tau, subscript b for ordinal data (Disbrow, personal communication). The results showed significant negative correlations between the F-E scale and child abuse, as well as between the F-E scale and other predictors including an 80-item attitude scale for parents and the home interview scale. The Mach IV scale also correlated positively with child abuse. In this sample there was a significant negative correlation between the Mach IV scale and the F-E scale, contrary to results reported earlier in this chapter from a college student sample.

When data collection was finished for the 179 subjects in Disbrow's sample, results had been compiled on 1122 test items, in addition to the physiological responses. The data were reduced by means of a program of statistical analysis designated "path analysis" (Duncan, 1966), which involves mapping paths among sets of relationships between variables. Contrary to the results in the preliminary analysis, none of the five empathy scales emerged as a significant predictor of child abuse. In the process of data reduction, therefore, the five empathy scales were combined. The three F-E items were retained with minor changes in wording, and the scale was supplemented with nine questions correlating with child abuse taken from the other four empathy scales, forming a new 12-item scale (see Table 7-6, Appendix D). Included in the new scale were three items from the denial-avoidance scale including: "One should not get too involved in other people's problems;" and three from the hostility scale including: "If my friends get poor grades, that's their problem." There were also three items from the other two simple empathy scales: involvement-concern and friend empathy.

Similar scaling techniques were used to reduce the number of questions and to improve internal consistency of the attitude scales, and factor analysis was used to reduce the interview questions. The resulting 28 indicators and 12 physiological variables were further cut down by use of discriminant analysis (Morrison, 1969). The final 17 indicators, including the 12-item empathy scale, were identified as those which best discriminated between abusers and nonabusers in the sample.

Results of the physiological measures taken during the film viewing indicate some of the problems involved in analyzing behavior of low empathizers. Heart rate responses of the sample of child abusers and neglectors showed no significant variation across pleasant and unpleasant scenes and there were no "orienting responses" registered by this group, as contrasted with the controls. This significant difference between the two groups was interpreted to indicate that abusers and neglectors were not attending to the filmed scenes.

Validation of Dr. Disbrow's 19 predictors of child abuse will be carried out on a new sample of known abusers and controls in a four-year longitudinal study of patients from a health maintenance organization. Data from this new study should show some indication as to whether adding items to the F-E scale will improve its reliability and validity, and whether it is possible to find measures to test the personality correlates of low empathizers.

NOTE

1. Hansson suggested that the Mach IV scale, unlike the F-E and Wrightsman instruments, contains an element of behavioral intention or willingness to use given interpersonal strategies, which could explain the lack of relationship.

Chapter 8

SELF PERCEPTION:

EMPATHY AND ANDROGYNY

Reporting research by Robert O. Hansson,
Mary E. Chernovetz, and Warren H. Jones

A picture of the empathetic individual, the high scorer on the F-E scale, has begun to emerge. In social interactions, such individuals tend to imagine themselves in the position of the other person and to feel the other's emotions as their own. Individual differences, including birth order, interact with situational variables to govern the occurrence of empathetic identification and its target, but it has been shown that high fantasizers tend to perceive other people in general as more variable and complex than nonempathizers do, and to be less prone to make negative generalizations about others.

If the self concept is formed by identification with other people, as is assumed by personality theorists of a wide variety of orientations, then high fantasizers should be more variable than others in their self concepts, just as they have learned to see others as more variable and complex. This hypothesis still remains to be tested, but a recent study by Hansson, Chernovetz, and Jones (1975) at the University of Tulsa on sex role perceptions of high and low empathizers tends to support the relationship between empathy and variability in self perception.

The challenge to sex role stereotypes by the women's movement during the last decade has given rise to a number of self-report instruments designed to measure sex-typed traits incorporated into the self concept (Broverman et al., 1972). As early as 1968, Rosenkrantz et al. (1968) designed a bi-polar instrument in which respondents rated themselves on traits which had been scaled as typical masculine or feminine characteristics. More recently, Sandra Bem has developed the theoretical concept of the androgynous individual, defined as one capable of engaging comfortably in both masculine and femine-typed behaviors. Bem's self-report scale, the Bem Sex Role Inventory (BSRI) (Bem, 1974), purports to measure the degree to which an individual perceives him/herself as sex-typed or androgynous. In the Hansson et al. study, scores on Bem's instrument were correlated with F-E scale scores to test the prediction that high fantasizers would be less sex-typed than lows in their self perceptions.

The Androgyny Scale

The BSRI contains 60 personality characteristics previously scaled as being desirable masculine, feminine, or neutral characteristics. Subjects are asked to indicate on a seven-point scale the extent to which each trait is "true of me." The BSRI is then scored by calculating the subject's total masculine score and total feminine score and subtracting the feminine from the masculine score. In this manner, subjects may be viewed as sex-typed (i.e., masculine males and feminine females), opposite sex-typed (feminine males and masculine females), or androgynous (reflecting a somewhat equal endorsement of masculine and feminine traits). Bem and her associates have conducted several experiments on construct validation (Bem, 1975a, 1975b) indicating that androgynous individuals are freer to engage in and to enjoy certain behaviors typed as masculine and feminine.

How is androgyny related to empathy? Because many personality traits popularly associated with empathy tend to be seen as "feminine" (e.g., Bem's traits labeled "understanding" and "sensitive to the needs of others"), one possibility is that sex-typed females and cross-sex typed males would constitute the high empathizers. Research on the F-E scale, however, led Hansson et al. to a different approach. They predicted that high F-Es, who tend to enter imaginatively into many roles, would not experience discomfort with a self concept and behavior not conventionally sex-typed. Thus, it was hypothesized that scores on the F-E scale would be negatively correlated with sex-typing on the BSRI.

Subjects were 179 college students who earned extra credit in their psychology classes for participation. All subjects completed the F-E scale and the BSRI.

Scores on the test were divided into six groups for analysis on the basis of sex-type and sex. The BSRI is scored by computing the t-ratio for each subject for the differences between responses to the 20 masculine and 20 feminine traits on the scale. The t-ratio is then considered an index of the extent to which a subject is masculine, androgynous, or feminine. Bem's research to date has identified as androgynous those whose responses to the masculine items of the BSRI were not significantly different from their responses to the feminine items (at $p < .05$ significance level). It is on this basis that the figure of 35 percent androgynous was established (Bem, 1974). She noted, however, that use of the .05 significance level was an arbitrary scheme, and suggested that future researchers establish classification categories appropriate to the distribution of t-scores in their own samples. Accordingly, subjects in the Hansson study were classified as follows: subjects with a t-ratio of > 1.0 were classified masculine, subjects with a t-ratio between

1.0 and —1.0 were classified androgynous, and those with a t-ratio < —1.0 were classified feminine.

In order to determine the effects of sex and sex-type on subjects' scores on the F-E scale, a 2 x 3 ANOVA was performed on the data. The expected main effect for sex-type was obtained (F = 4.36, df = 2/173, p < .05). Subjects who were less sex-typed generally did score higher on the F-E scale. There was no significant main effect for sex and no interaction effect. (Mean empathy scores for the six groups are presented in Table 8-1, Appendix D, and the summary ANOVA is presented in Table 8-2.)

The failure to find sex differences in empathy scores is interesting in view of the results in the first validation of the F-E scale reported in Chapter 2. An analysis of the relationship between sex-type and F-E score in this study shows that among female subjects this was straightforward. Opposite sex-typed females had significantly higher empathy scores than sex-type females (t = 2.66, df = 63, p < .01). The relationship among male subjects was less straightforward. Opposite sex-typed males did have the highest empathy scores among male subjects, significantly higher than androgynous males (t = 1.95, df = 34, p < 05). However, the total here was small, only 9 out of 77 male subjects. Furthermore, androgynous males (N = 27) had lower empathy scores than sex-typed males, although the difference did not reach statistical significance.

The findings in Hansson et al.'s study, then, supported the hypothesis that the freedom to be comfortable with an "inappropriate" self concept and "inappropriate" role behaviors is associated with high scores on the F-E scale. This gives some support to the earlier finding that high F-Es see themselves, as well as other people, as more variable and complex. Only for high F-E opposite males where the two predictors coincide is the conventional notion of femininity-empathy supported. At the same time these findings raise some questions about the self concepts of high fantasizers which can only be answered by further research. Although there were no sex differences in F-E scores, there were differences, based on sex, in the self concepts of high fantasizers. Why do empathizing females, more than males, tend toward androgyny and cross-sex typing? One possible explanation focuses on the choice of persons with whom to identify and empathize. In the laboratory under controlled conditions where it is possible to focus on the object of empathy, it has been shown that both situational variables and such individual differences as birth order determine empathetic reactions (see Chapter 1). On a theoretical level, Stotland has related these different reactions to the different social schemas that govern the behavior of the first-and-only children and later borns.

Social schema theory also offers a possible explanation for the different reactions of males and females in the Hansson et al. study. Considering the long history of sexual inequality in our culture, it seems likely that one prevalent higher-order schema would relate the dimension of masculinity to power and social approval. Such a schema might determine behavior of both males and females in choosing identification models. For example, in the plays, novels, or movies in which a high fantasizer may have chosen to identify with the role of another, the masculine characters are usually the most exciting, interesting, and socially approved (see Russ, 1972). Furthermore, personality characteristics ascribed to men are generally higher valued in our society (Broverman et al., 1972: 75). Clearly, all things being equal, high fantasizers probably have more experience in playing the male role.

For males, then, there is very little incentive to choose members of the opposite sex with whom to identify, which would account for the fact that high fantasizing males were as likely to be sex-typed as to be androgynous. For a woman, choosing a role model may be more complex. Particularly for later borns, the dimension of similarity has been shown to be an important factor in empathetic responding. Although no birth order differences emerged from Hansson's data, it seems possible that many later-born women would tend to empathize in a same-sex dimension. However, not all women, fictional or real, fit the feminine stereotype, and high fantasizers might find more salient a woman with some characteristics stereotyped as masculine. Women who identify with other women and who are also high fantasizers might develop, through identification, a personality of the type Bem terms androgynous.

Chapter 9

FANTASY-EMPATHY RESEARCH:

AN INTEGRATION

Erza Stotland

In these final pages, my intent is both to summarize and to attempt to integrate the findings of the studies reported in this volume. In addition, other studies relevant to the present series will be discussed. The focus will be the fantasy-empathy (F-E) scale, but the reader should bear in mind that several other scales emerged from the factor analysis of the large pool of items (Chapter 2). The validity and reliability of these other scales were not tested, primarily because of the practical limitations of the setting in which the studies were done. For example, the friend-empathy scale could have been validated only with the use of friends as the objects of empathy. Furthermore, the length of the other scales precluded using them in the Crisis Clinic study. In fact, one of the features of the F-E scale which might have helped validate it is that the items refer to empathizing with "strangers," i.e., characters in plays, novels, etc. In the validation studies the objects of identification were all "strangers."

The F-E Scale: Reliability

The test-retest reliability of the F-E scale is indicated in the work of Mathews (reported in Chapter 2) in which the uncorrected reliability coefficient was .83. For a three-item scale, the reliability of such scores is remarkable. The internal consistency of the scale is indicated in several ways. The consistency of the scale is attested to by the factor analysis (Chapter 2) in which all of the three items loaded .55 or better on the common factor. The relatively heavy loading on the items should not be surprising in view of the fact that they all refer to empathizing with fictional characters. Obviously the reliability and usefulness of the scale in research and for selection would be greatly enhanced by adding more items: a three-item scale is almost a misnomer. But any additional items would have to retain the homogeneity of the present scale. If this homgeneity is retained, then a point of diminishing returns might soon be reached. Additional items might not add enough discrimination to the scale to make the added work and time worthwhile. In any case, most researchers would have to admit that a good, i.e., valid, one-item scale is better than a scale of questionable validity.

The "purity" of the scale is indicated also by its independence of other scales and their correlated traits. Nevertheless, one trait which might be thought to contaminate the scale is the tendency to give socially desirable answers, because empathy is sometimes described as a desirable trait in human society. However, the scale was found to be unrelated to the Marlowe-Crowne scale of social desirability, which is a well-validated measure of the tendency to act in a socially desirable way (Chapter 7), and to the Edwards social desirability scale (Chapter 2). Perhaps the indirectness of the items with respect to the process of emotional empathy itself may have disguised the items sufficiently so that the social desirability was not a salient factor. The purity of the scale is also indicated by the lack of any significant correlation with the California F scale (see Chapter 2) and with the Machiavellianism scale in a college student population (see Chapter 7). In both cases, negative correlations might have been expected because high authoritarians and high Machiavellians would be expected to empathize less. Perhaps there is a relationship between these scales and the F-E scale, but of a more subtle and complex type. This is suggested by the finding in a recent study that in a sample of child abusers the expected negative relationship between F-E and Machiavellianism appeared (Chapter 6). In the experimental work on empathy reported by Stotland, Sherman, and Shaver (1971) and discussed in Chapter 1, birth order was found to be a factor determining the conditions under which a person empathized, although it could not be concluded that birth order groups differ across the board in the degree of empathy. Consistent with these results, scores on the F-E scale have not been found to be related to birth order.

There is some indication that women score higher on the F-E scale than men (Chapter 2), but the tendency is not confirmed in other studies (Chapters 7 and 8). To the extent that sex differences are confirmed by other studies, the differences might reflect women finding it more socially desirable, or more in conformity with their traditional roles to report that they empathize more. However, the study by Hansson et al. (Chapter 8) suggests that the high F-E female is less likely than other women to view her own sex role in the traditional mold.

One other relationship that should be noted is that between the F-E scale and Elms' fantasy scale (Elms, 1966), from which two of the three items in the F-E scale are derived. A desired characteristic of any psychological test, in addition to reliability and validity, is its discriminate validity. Campbell and Fiske (1959) have indicated that a reliable and valid test may be of little value if it lacks discrimination, that is, if it is too highly correlated with existing tests. In this regard Mathews (Chapter 2) found that when the two overlapping items were subtracted from the scores of subjects on Elms' scale, the correlations in his two samples with the F-E scale were .47 (n = 44) and .30 (N = 49).

Although these correlations are significant (p < .05), the relationship is low enough to conclude that the two scales are in fact measuring different aspects of the same trait of fantasy: in the case of Elms' scale, the tendency to engage in fantasy in general; and in the case of the F-E scale, the tendency to engage in empathetic fantasy. One might further argue that the obtained relationship between the two scales is inflated by similar method factors, i.e., same stimulus presentation format and same response indication.

The F-E Scale: Validity

We turn now to the central problem of the validity of the scale. A person who tends to place himself imaginatively in the position of another individual would be expected to learn more about the feelings of other people than someone who does this less frequently. Of course the accuracy of what the first person learns of the other's experience depends on the accuracy of his imagination. Nonetheless, in a situation in which the other's role and experiences are partially clear, a person high on the F-E scale would be expected to learn more about the other person than the person who is low on the F-E scale. One situation in which the other person's experiences are made clear is when his role is actually enacted, as in Elms' 1966 study in which smokers enacted the role of trying to persuade another person to stop smoking. High F-E people would be expected to learn more of the arguments and of their overtones and implications than low F-Es when enacting the role. Because health is a positive value for most people, the higher F-E person would be likely to take heed of what he had learned while enacting the role. This expectation is confirmed by the finding that two items of the F-E scale which were borrowed from Elms' scale both correlate in the expected direction with the amount of attitude change toward smoking three months later. This finding has subsequently been confirmed by Matefy (1972). (The third item in the F-E scale was not used in the Elms scale.)

Because high F-E people apparently tend to learn more from these experiences, it would be expected that on the whole they would have more additional bits of knowledge about "other people in general" than low F-E individuals. Because there are few overall statements about "other people in general" that are valid because of the great variation of people due to individual differences, high F-E people tend to be more aware of these differences and to describe people as heterogeneous (Chapter 7). The high F-E's recognition of the variability of others would also be expected to lead to greater appreciation and acceptance of variation in types of human beings, thus making such individuals less likely to stereotype members of minority groups (Chapter 7). Here we make the assumption that the differences among people that are perceived by high F-E scorers are not threatening to them. As we shall see below, some differences might be threatening to them, but this threat is probably mitigated by the fact, also cited below, that high F-E people tend to assume that people in general are more altruistic than do low F-E people (see Chapter 7).

As reported in Stotland, Sherman and Shaver (1971) and Aderman and Berkowitz (1970), imagining oneself in another person's painful situation has been experimentally determined to lead to one's experiencing negative affect, i.e., to simple emotional empathy. In the Stotland research, this empathy was manifested in physiological reactions such as palmar sweating, as well as in subjective expression. Because high F-E people are more prone to imagine themselves in another's position, it is not unexpected that they have been found to show more palmar sweat or more vasoconstriction and more negative subjective reactions when observing another person experiencing pain than do low F-E people. This was found in (a) the validity study (Chapter 2) in which they observed a person undergoing a painful diathermy machine treatment (although this was found only for vasoconstriction); (b) in the research reported in Chapter 3 in which they also observed someone undergoing this type of treatment (palmar sweat only); and (c) in Chapter 4 where nursing students observed a film of the death of a patient in a

hospital. These studies show that the F-E scale is in fact correlated with emotional empathy, a key to the validation of the
scale, even though the variations in the physiological system
reflecting emotion remain unexplained.

Fantasy-Empathy and Helping Others

Thus far we have shown the cognitive and emotional effects of
high fantasy-empathy. It remains now to show that these cognitive and emotional responses influence overt behavior. A
common sense assumption one might make is that high empathy
leads to helping others who are in pain and suffering. Empathy
is often spoken of as a prerequisite for people who enter the
helping professions. However, this issue has to be examined a
bit more analytically and considered in the light of recent research on altruistic behavior. A person who is empathizing with
a suffering other will no doubt be motivated to reduce his own
empathized negative emotion. One way he can do so is to reduce
the suffering of the other, i.e., to help the other. Weiss et al.
(1971; 1973), as described in Chapter 1, demonstrated that
people will learn an instrumental conditioned response, the
reinforcer for which is the deliverance of another person from
painful electric shocks. Whether the empathizer will choose to
reduce his own pain by helping the other person is influenced
by at least several factors: (a) the individual's perception that he
can, in fact, help the other; and the extent to which the individual perceives himself to be a competent helper in the situation; and (b) the individual's perception that he is responsible
for the other's welfare. The second factor is illustrated in a study
by Geer and Jarmecky (1973) using an experimental paradigm
similar to that of Weiss et al. (1971), in which college students
observed another receiving painful shock. It was found that for
the observers who believed that the faster their own response,
the less shock was delivered to the model, reaction time was
faster than for subjects who were not led to feel responsibility
for relieving the pain of the model.

The interaction of the factors of perceived competence and
responsibility is illustrated in the hospital study (Chapter 5),

where it was found that those nursing students who were first born and only children and who were also high on F-E spent 86 percent of their time in the patient's room during the last four weeks of the eight-week hospital training, while they spent only 31 percent during the first four weeks. No doubt the student nurses felt some responsibility for the patients, but at the same time they were probably uncertain of what to do for them in the early part of the study. Because first borns tend to rely on their own resources less than later borns do in times of stress (Schachter, 1959), they were less likely to stay in the patient's room where they were on their own. Later on, when they became more self-confident or had received psychological support, they vastly increased the time spent in the rooms, more so than any other group.

A direct relationship between empathy and helping has been found in studies using measures of empathy other than the F-E scale. (It should be kept in mind throughout the discussion that no assumption is made that empathy is the only determinant of altruistic or helping behavior. Many other motivations may be described such as norms of responsibility, social norms, instructions, etc., c.f. Macaulay and Berkowitz, 1970.)

Liebhart (1972) measured his subjects' tendency toward "sympathetic orientation" by means of a measure devised by Lenrow (1965). In this measure, subjects are presented with an unemotional description of a series of conflict situations between a person's suffering and some rule of society. For example, one description was summarized as follows: "An itinerant farm worker with a large family to move . . . is permitted to steal a truck by a police observer." Subjects were then asked to describe each of the situations in their own words using their imaginations to recapture what the scenes were in real life. The protocols were then content-analyzed for the use of emotional words showing:

1. favorable orientation to the person in need . . . 2. use of the first person narrative expressing the subjective experience of the person in need . . . and 3. descriptive elaboration on the subjective experience of the person in need.

The latter two content analytic categories appear to overlap with what the F-E scale purports to measure, although the first category of favorable orientation does not. Liebhart used the measure in an experimental setting in which the subject was led by means of screams and a moan to believe that another expeimental subject in an adjoining room had just suffered an injury. Subjects who were high in sympathetic orientation tended to help the other subject sooner than did those low in sympathetic orientation. Liebhart also found that subjects who had indicated more willingness to act to help themselves in emergencies attempted help sooner than those who indicated that they were less likely to help themselves. Thus people who are both empathetic and oriented toward action are more likely to help others.

Another study which ties overt behavior to empathetic types of response is that of Schwartz (1970) (see Chapter 7). He gave his subjects an "awareness of consequences" measure, a projective test in which they described the feelings and thoughts which might run through the minds of persons who faced decisions involving interpersonal consequences. Schwartz also measured by questionnaire his subjects' tendency to assume responsibility for their own actions. As an outcome measure the subjects were asked to describe their own standards for personal behavior and the subjects' friends were asked to describe the former's overt behavior. The critical measure was the degree of correlation between these personal codes of conduct and actual conduct. Schwartz found that for subjects who were high on both awareness of consequences and in acceptance of personal responsibility, the correlation between their code of conduct and their actual behavior was higher than for those who were not high on both.

The basis of the development of tendencies to have fantasy empathy or "sympathetic orientation" or "awareness of consequences" is indicated in the work of Hoffman and Saltzstein (1967). They found that moral, i.e., considerate, behavior toward others occurred more among children whose parents pointed out the consequences of their behavior for the welfare of others, provided the parents had a warm relationship with the children.

These children were more considerate than those who were punished for wrong-doing or were simply told that a given action was "wrong." Notice that the warmth of the parent might have motivated the child to act appropriately in his knowledge of the consequences of his behavior.

Mehrabian and Epstein (1972) measured empathy by a questionnaire consisting of items designed to test the following:

> susceptibility to emotional contagion . . . ; appreciation of the feelings of unfamiliar and distant others . . . ; extreme emotional responsiveness (to others' feelings) . . . ; tendency to be moved by others' positive or negative emotional experiences . . . ; sympathetic tendency . . . ; and willingness to be in contact with others who have problems.

It can be seen that the content of the questionnaire overlapped to some degree with the F-E scale,[1] but also with some of the other scales developed by the factor analysis and described in Chapter 2. Mehrabian and Epstein related their broad measure of empathy to altruism and aggression. To measure altruism, they gave subjects a chance to help another student with no material reward for themselves. These researchers found that high empathy subjects helped more. To measure aggression, the subjects were given an opportunity to administer shocks to another subject in a "learning" study, with the magnitude of shocks controlled by the first subject. When the "erring subject" was in the same room with the actual subject, high empathy subjects administered less shock than did low empathizers. No difference between the two empathy groups was found when the "erring subjects" were in a different room.

In all the studies just cited, high empathy, however defined, was related to helping, consideration for others, and nonaggression, etc. However, these studies also showed that such altruistic behavior is also dependent on some form of motivational factor such as sense of responsibility, knowledge of what to do, a tendency to act instrumentally in general, permission from an experimenter, or a direct report from the other or from a warm parent. These findings suggest that emphathizing will not invariably lead to behavior which is beneficial to others.

In addition to the presence of empathy, then, certain motivational factors must be present to produce helping behavior. And in some instances these other motivating factors when combined with empathy may lead to higher levels of, or more effective, aggression. For example, Johnson (1967), studying aggression, found that previous practice of the role of an opponent led to more effective subsequent performance against him.

Furthermore, in the absence of ability or motivation to act to help the other, a highly empathetic person might escape from or avoid noxious, empathetically induced emotional states in other ways. He might withdraw from the other, either physically or psychologically. Physical withdrawal was clearly indicated in the student nurse study. Piliavin and Piliavin (1972) found that, if a person fell down in the subway and began to bleed at the mouth, passengers were less likely to help than if the victim did not bleed at the mouth. The passengers avoided physical proximity to a potentially empathetically disturbing situation, especially because it was unclear what could be done for the victim in the subway. Psychological withdrawal may be attempted when neither physical withdrawal nor constructive actions are possible. Lazarus et al. (1962; 1964; 1965), as reported in Chapter 1, illustrated the use of intellectualizing ego defenses which entail emotional withdrawal in reducing empathized pain while viewing stressful films, and it was also found (Lazarus, 1966) that people who characteristically employed this type of ego defense were low in terms of physiological arousal when viewing film scenes depicting pain. In the Mrs. Reynolds film study (Chapter 4), the high empathy nurses who identified very strongly with the patient in the film were also quite low in their emotional responsiveness as measured at the conclusion of the film.

Fantasy and Altruism

If one makes the assumption that in most situations in life a person can help others in distress, that he or she feels a responsibility for so doing, and that such help is socially desirable, it is likely that on the average high F-E people will in fact behave in more characteristically or chronically helpful ways than will low F-E people. We have no data to support this proposition directly. If we assume its veracity, however, we can more readily explain the Hansson findings in Chapter 7 that high F-E people tend to judge "people in general" as more altruistic. High F-Es may simply be generalizing from themselves to the world; they may engender more altruistic behavior in others by their own altruism, etc. Nevertheless, this tendency to perceive others as altruistic may be limited by the tendency cited above for high F-E people to learn more about the motivations of others. (The validity of this rather cynical comment needs to be checked by researchers.)

Furthermore, it may be that high F-Es are less likely to follow the pattern described by Lerner (1966) as reflecting motivation to see a "just world." This pattern leads one to see innocent victims of harm as deserving that harm. Aderman, Brehm and Katz (1974) found that instructing subjects to imagine themselves in the place of the victim led to reduced "just world" derogation of the victim (see Chapter 6). Thus, it might be expected that high F-E people engage in "just world" perceptions less than lows. This tendency would then help to explain the findings that high F-E people tend to perceive others somewhat more positively in general (Chapter 7).

Empathy and Birth Order

Throughout the work reported in the present volume and the previous work in this series (Stotland, 1969; Stotland et al., 1971), birth order has emerged as an important factor in the study of empathy. In the previous work, birth order was found to be a determinant of the social situations in which a person empathized, although there were no indications of overall differences between birth order groups in the amount of empathy. Likewise, in the present studies, no differences have been found in the F-E scores of first borns and onlies on the one hand and the later borns on the other.

We see, however, that high F-E plays different roles for the two birth order groups. For first and onlies, as shown in the hospital study, it tends to lead to avoidance of situations involving empathized pain unless the individual feels quite secure in the situation. Furthermore, some of the high F-E first and onlies found the nursing situation so difficult that they appeared to have a somewhat higher rate of dropping out of nursing school. Mathews (personal communication) found approximately two years after the completion of the hospital study (at which time the student nurses should have graduated) that there was a nonsignificant tendency for first and onlies to have either temporarily or permanently dropped out of the nursing program as a function of F-E scores. First and onlies who were low, moderate, or high on the F-E scale had the following dropout rates respectively: 10, 16.6, 22.2 percent. For later borns, the same respective rate was 22.7, 25.0, 23.0 percent. On the other hand, when the action required was relatively simple, Hammersla (1974) found that high F-E first and onlies were more likely than later borns to help a distraught stranger (Chapter 6).

For later borns, high F-E appears to lead to greater helpfulness when such help can be given, as in the hospital study where high F-E later borns showed the tendency to spend more time in the patients' rooms than did lows during the first four weeks. Referring back to the consistent finding reported in Stotland (1969) and Stotland et al. (1971) that this group tends to empathize more with people who are similar to them than with those who are different, it can be predicted that they would also be more likely to help another who is perceived as similar, although this prediction has not been tested. As shown in Chapter 7, later borns high in F-E do appear to reject people who are different from them in attitude, possibly because they understand what attitudes others hold better than do those low in F-E. It is improtant to recognize that the rejection of differences involves attitudes and beliefs rather than ethnic differences, because high F-E people tend to be less likely to make negative generalizations about people of other races, regardless of birth order (Chapter 7).

Conclusions

In sum, the research reported appears to show that the F-E scale is a reliable measure of the tendency to place oneself imaginatively in the role of another. The validity of the scale has been shown by the relationship between scores on the scale and a number of variables: learning about others' experience by playing their roles, being emotionally aroused in the presence of distraught others, and being less willing to downgrade minority groups. There were also some slight indications that when a high F-E person feels that he can help another to relieve his suffering he will do so, but most of the evidence of the relationship between empathy and helping comes from other, related studies. However, when a high F-E person finds himself in a situation in which he feels unable to help a distraught other with whom he might empathize, he tends to avoid or escape the situation either physically or psychologically. Birth order also appears to influence the reactions of high empathy people; first borns and onlies tend to escape noxious empathy-induced emotions while later borns tend to help another who is distraught.

Obviously, much further work needs to be done on the F-E scale. The number of items needs to be increased. The hypothesized complex relationship to helping needs to be verified. Relationships to liking for others and to perception of the self and of others need to be studied. And the source in previous experience for high and low F-E scores needs to be determined.

NOTE

1. Hammersla (1974) found a moderate but significant correlation of .47 between the F-E scale and the Mehrabian and Epstein questionnaire (see Chapter 6).

REFERENCES

ACKNER, B. (1956) "Emotions and the peripheral vasoconstriction system." *Journal of Psychosomatic Research* 1: 3-20.

ADERMAN, D. and L. BERKOWITZ (1970) "Observational set, empathy, and helping." *Journal of Personality and Social Psychology* 14: 141-148.

ADERMAN, D., S. BREHM, and L. B. KATZ (1974) "Empathetic observation of an innocent victim: the just world revisited." *Journal of Personality and Social Psychology* 29, No. 3: 342-347.

ALFERT, E. (1966) "Comparison of responses to a vicarious and direct threat." *Journal of Experimental Research in Personality* 1: 179-186.

ARONFREED, J. (1968) *Conduct and Conscience: The Socialization of Internalized Control Over Behavior.* New York: Academic Press.

——— and V. PASKAL (1968) "Altruism, empathy and the conditioning of positive affect." Reported in J. Aronfreed, *Conduct and Conscience.* New York: Academic Press.

BANDURA, A. and T. L. ROSENTHAL (1966) "Vicarious classical conditioning as a function of arousal level." *Journal of Personality and Social Psychology* 3, No. 1: 54-62.

BARON, R. A. (1971a) "Magnitude of victim's pain cues and level of prior anger arousal as determinants of adult aggressive behavior." *Journal of Personality and Social Psychology* 17: 236-243.

——— (1971b) "Aggression as a function of magnitude of victim's pain cues, level of prior anger arousal, and aggressor-victim similarity." *Journal of Personality and Social Psychology* 18: 48-54.

BEAM, J. C. (1955) "Serial learning and conditioning under real-life stress." *Journal of Abnormal and Social Psychology* 51: 543-551.

BEM, S. L. (1974) "The measurement of psychological androgyny." *Journal of Consulting and Clinical Psychology* 42: 155-162.

——— (1975a) "Sex role adaptability: one consequence of psychological androgyny." *Journal of Personality and Social Psychology* 31, No. 4: 634-643.

——— (1975b) "Fluffy women and chesty men." *Psychology Today* (September): 58-62.

BERGER, S. M. (1962) "Conditioning through vicarious instigation." *Psychological Review* 69: 450-466.

BLEDA, P. R. (1976) "Empathy, sympathy and altruism." *JSAS Catalog of Selected Documents in Psychology,* MS 1180, 6: 9.

BORKE, H. (1971) "Interpersonal perception of young children: egocentrism or empathy?" *Developmental Psychology* 5: 263-269.

BORING, E. G. (1957) *A History of Experimental Psychology.* New York: Appleton-Century-Crofts.

BROVERMAN, I. K., S. R. VOGEL, D. M. BROVERMAN, F. E. CLARKSON, and P. S. ROSENKRANTZ (1972) "Sex-role stereotypes: a current appraisal." *Journal of Social Issues* 28: 59-78.

BUSS, A. H. (1966a) "The effect of harm on subsequent aggression." *Journal of Experimental Research on Personality* 1: 249-255.

——— (1966b) "Instrumentality of aggression, feedback and frustration as determinants of physical aggression." *Journal of Personality and Social Psychology* 3: 153-162.

BYRNE, D. (1966) *An Introduction to Personality: A Research Approach.* Englewood Cliffs, N.J.: Prentice-Hall.

——— (1969) "Attitudes and attraction." In L. Berkowitz (ed.), *Advances in Experimental Social Social Psychology* Vol. 4. New York: Academic Press.

——— (1971) *The Attraction Paradigm.* New York: Academic Press.

CAMPBELL, D. T. and D. FISKE "Convergent and discriminant validation by multitrait-multimethod matrix." *Psychological Bulletin* 4, No. 1: 36-43.

CHANDLER, M. and S. GREENSPAN (1972) "Ersatz egocentrism: a reply to H. Borke." *Developmental Psychology* 2: 104-106.

CHINSKY, J. M and J. RAPPAPORT (1970) "Brief critique of the meaning and reliability of accurate empathy rating." *Psychological Bulletin* 73: 379-382.

CHRISTIE, R. and F. L. GEIS (1970) *Studies in Machiavellianism.* New York: Academic Press.

CLINE, V. B. and J. M. RICHARDS, Jr. (1960) "Accuracy of interpersonal perception: a general trait?" *Journal of Abnormal and Social Psychology* 60: 20-30.

CRAWFORD, R., E. STOTLAND, and K. SHAVER (1967) Set-up for obtaining plethysmographic recordings from several subjects simultaneously." *Psychophysiology* 3: 435-439.

CRONBACH, L. J. (1955) "Processes affecting scores on 'understanding of others' and 'assumed similarity.'" *Psychological Bulletin* 52: 177-193.

DARLEY, J. M. and B. LATANE (1968) "Bystander intervention in emergencies: diffusion of responsibility." *Journal of Personality and Social Psychology* 8: 377-383.

DAVIS, L. K., R. O. HANSSON, and W. H. JONES (1975) Unpublished manuscript, University of Tulsa, Oklahoma.

DAVIS, R. C., A. M. BUCHWALD, and R. W. FRANKMAN (1955) "Autonomic and muscular responses and their relations to simple stimuli. *Psychological Monographs* 69: (9, whole no. 405).

DAVIS, R. H. (1957) "Critique and notes: a further study of the effect of stress on palmar prints." *Journal of Abnormal and Social Psychology* 55: 132.

DiLOLLO, V. and S. M. BERGER (1965) "Effects of apparent pain in others on observers' reaction time." *Journal of Personality and Social Psychology* 2: 573-575.

DISBROW, M. A., H. O. DOERR, and C. CAULFIELD (1977) "Measures to predict child abuse." Department of Maternal and Child Nursing, Univ. of Washington, Seattle.

DUNCAN, O. D. (1966) "Path analysis: sociological examples." *American Journal of Sociology* 72: 1-16.

DYMOND, R. F. (1949) "A scale for measurement of empathetic ability." *Journal of Consulting Psychology* 14: 127-133.

——— (1950) "Personality and empathy." *Journal of Consulting Psychology* 14: 343-350.

EFRAYMSEN, M. A. (1960) "Multiple regression analysis." In A. Ralston and H. S. Wolf (eds.), *Mathematical Methods for Digital Computers* Part 5 (17). New York: John Wiley.

EIKSTEIN, R. (1972) "Psychoanalysis and education for the facilitation of positive human qualities." *Journal of Social Issues* 28, No. 3: 71-85.

ELMS, A. C. (1966) "Influence of fantasy-empathy on attitude change through role playing." *Journal of Abnormal and Social Psychology* 4, No. 1: 36-43.

FENICHEL, O. (1945) *The Psychoanalytic Theory of Neurosis.* New York: W. W. Norton.

FERREIRA, A. J. and W. D. WINTER (1963) "The palmar sweat print: a methodological study." *Psychosomatic Medicine* 25: 377-384.

FESHBACH, N. D. (1973) "Empathy: an interpersonal process." Paper presented at the American Psychological Association, Montreal.

FESTINGER, L., S. SCHACHTER, and K. BACK (1950) *Social Pressures in Informal Groups: A Study of Human Factors in Housing.* New York: Harper and Row.

FLAVELL, J. H., P. T. BOTKIN, C. L. FRY, J. W. WRIGHT, and P. E. JARVIS (1968) *The Development of Role-Taking and Communication Skills in Children.* New York: John Wiley.

GAGE, N. L. and L. G. CRONBACH (1955) "Conceptual and methodological problems in interpersonal perception." *Psychological Review* 62: 411-423.

GEER, J. H. and L. JARMECKY (1973) "The effect of being responsible for reducing another's pain on subject's response and arousal." *Journal of Personality and Social Psychology* 232-237.

GILL, B. (1975) "A painful case." *New Yorker* (July 7), 63.

GLADSTONE, R. (1953) "A group test of palmar sweating." *Journal of General Psychology* 48: 29-49.

HAMMERSLA, E. J. (1974) "The effects of participation in a laboratory bystander intervention study on subsequent attitudes and intervention behavior." Unpublished doctoral dissertation, Univ. of Washington, Seattle.

HANSSON, R. O., M. E. CHERNOVETZ, and L. K. DAVIS (1975) Unpublished manuscript, University of Tulsa, Oklahoma.

HARRISON, A. (1969) "Exposure and popularity." *Journal of Personality* 37: 359-377.

HASTORF, A. H., I. E. BENDER, and D. J. WEINTRAUB (1955) "The influence of response patterns on the 'refined empathy score.'" *Journal of Abnormal and Social Psychology* 51: 341-343.

HATCH, R. S. (1962) "An evaluation of a forced-choice differential accuracy approach to the measurement of supervisory empathy." *Dissertation Abstracts* 23: 323.

HOFFMAN, M. and H. SALTZSTEIN (1967) "Parent discipline and the child's moral development." *Journal of Personality and Social Psychology* 5: 45-67.

HOVLAND, C. and A. RIESEN (1940) "Magnitude of galvanic and vasomotor responses as a function of stimulus intensity." *Journal of General Psychology* 23: 103-121.

IANNOTTI, R. J. and J. A. MEACHAM (1974) "The nature, measurement and development of empathy." Paper presented at the meeting of the Eastern Psychological Association, Philadelphia.

JENSEMA, C. "MISSTEP: a stepwise multiple regression analysis program." Unpublished paper, Univ. of Washington Counseling and Testing Bureau, Seattle.

JOHNSON, D. W. (1967) "Use of role reversal in mitigating competition." *Journal of Personality and Social Psychology* 7: 135-141.

KAISER, H. F. (1958) "The varimax criterion for analytic rotation in factor analysis." *Psychometrika* 23: 187-200.

KATZ, R. L. (1963) *Empathy: Its Nature and Uses.* Glencoe, Ill.: Free Press.

KERR, W. A. and B. J. SPEROFF (1951) *The Empathy Test: Supplement to the Manual.* Chicago: Psychometric Affiliates.

KREBS, D. (1975) "Empathy and altruism." *Journal of Personality and Social Psychology* 32, No. 6: 1134-1146.

KUNO, Y. (1956) *Human Perspiration.* Springfield, Ill.: C. C. Thomas.

LACEY, J. J. (1950) "Individual differences in somatic response patterns." *Journal of Comparative and Physiological Psychology* 43: 338-350.

LAZARUS, R. S. (1966) *Psychological Stress and the Coping Process.* New York: McGraw-Hill.

——— , J. C. SPEISMAN, A. M. MORDKOFF, and L. A. DAVISON (1962) "A laboratory study of psychological stress produced by a motion picture film." *Psychological Monographs* 76, No. 34 (whole no. 553).

LAZARUS, R. S. and E. ALFERT (1964) "Short circuiting of threat by experimentally altering cognitive appraisal." *Journal of Abnormal and Social Psychology* 69: 195-205.

LAZARUS, R. S., E. M. OPTON, M. S. NOMIKOS, and N. O. RANKIN (1965) "The principle of short-circuiting of threat: further evidence." *Journal of Personality* 33: 622-635.

LENROW, P. (1965) "Studies in sympathy." in S. S. Tomkins and C. E. Izard (eds.), *Affect, Cognition and Personality: Empirical Studies.* New York: Springer.

LERNER, M. J. and C. H. SIMMONS (1966) "Observer's reaction to the 'innocent victim': compassion or rejection?" *Journal of Personality and Social Psychology* 4: 203-210.

LIEBHART, E. H. (1972) "Empathy and emergency helping: the effects of personality, self-concern, and acquaintance." *Journal of Experimental Social Psychology* 8: 404-411.

MACAULAY, J. and L. BERKOWITZ eds. (1970) *Altruism and Helping Behavior.* New York: Academic Press.

McDOUGALL, W. (1950) *An Introduction to Social Psychology.* London: Menthuen.

MAHONEY, S. C. (1960) "The literature empathy tests: development of a procedure for differentiating between 'good empathizers' and 'poor empathizers.'" *Dissertation Abstracts* 21: 674.

MARLOWE, D and D. P CROWNE (1961) "Social desirability and response to perceived situational demands." *Journal of Consulting Psychology* 25: 109-115.

MARQUIS, D. C. and D. J. WILLIAMS (1938) "The central pathway in man of the vasomotor response to pain. *Brain* 61: 203-220.

MATEFY, R. E. (1972) "Attitude change induced by role playing as a function of improvisation and role-taking ability." *Journal of Personality and Social Psychology* 24: 343-350.

MEAD, G. H. (1934) *Mind, Self and Society.* Chicago: Univ. of Chicago Press.

MEHRABIAN, A. and N. EPSTEIN (1972) "A measure of emotional empathy." *Journal of Personality* 40: 425-543.

MILGRAM, S. (1965) "Some conditions of obedience and disobedience to authority." *Human Relations* 18: 57-76.

MORRISON, D. G. (1969) "On the interpretation of discriminant analysis." *Journal of Marketing Research* 6: 156-163.

MOWRER, O. H. (1953) *Psychotherapy: Theory and Research.* New York: Ronald Press.

NAFE, J. P. and K. S. WAGONER (1936) "The effect of thermal stimulation upon dilation and constriction of the blood vessels of the skin of a contralateral hand." *Journal of Psychology* 2: 461-477.

——— (1938) "The effect of pain upon peripheral blood volume." *American Journal of Psychology* 51: 118-126.

NASON, S. (1970) "Clientele of Seattle Crisis Clinic, 1968." Unpublished Master of Social Work thesis, Univ. of Washington, Seattle.

ORNE, M. T. (1962) "On the social psychology of the psychological experiment: with particular reference to demand characteristics and their implications." *American Psychologist* 17: 776-783.

PIAGET, J. (1932) *The Moral Judgment of the Child.* New York: Harcourt, Brace and World.

PILIAVIN, I. M., J. RODIN, and J. A. PILIAVIN (1969) "Good Samaritanism: an underground phenomenon?" *Journal of Personality and Social Psychology* 13: 289-299.

PILIAVIN, J. A. and I. M. PILIAVIN (1972) "The effect of blood on reactions to a victim." *Journal of Personality and Social Psychology* 23: 235-261.

RAPPAPORT, J. and J. M. CHINSKY (1972) "Accurate empathy: confusion of a construct." *Psychological Bulletin* 77: 400-404.

ROGERS, C. R. (1957) "The necessary and sufficient conditions of therapeutic personality change." *Journal of Consulting Psychology* 21: 95-103.

——— (1967) *Person to Person.* Lafayette, Calif.: Real People Press.

ROSENKRANTZ, P. S., S. R. VOGEL, H. BEE, I. K. BROVERMAN, and D. M. BROVERMAN (1968) "Sex-role stereotypes and self-concepts in college students." *Journal of Consulting and Clinical Psychology* 32: 287-295.

ROTTER, J. B. (1966) "Generalized expectancies for internal versus external control of reinforcement." *Psychological Monographs* 80 (whole No. 609).

RUSS, J. (1972) "What can a heroine do? or why women can't write." In S. F. Cornillon (ed.), *Images of Women in Fiction: Feminist Perspectives.* Bowling Green, Ohio: B.G.W. Popular Press.

SARASON, I. (1958) "Interrelationships among individual difference variables, behavior in psychotherapy, and verbal conditioning." *Journal of Abnormal and Social Psychology* 56: 339-344.

SCHACHTER, S. (1959) *The Psychology of Affiliation: Experimental Studies of Gregariousness.* Stanford, Calif.: Stanford Univ. Press.

——— (1964) "The interaction of cognitive and physiological determinants of emotional state." In L. Berkowitz (ed.), *Advances in Experimental Social Psychology,* Vol. 1. New York: Academic Press.

SCHWARTZ, S. H. (1968) "Awareness of consequences and the influence of moral norms on interpersonal behavior." *Sociometry* 31: 355-369.

——— (1970) "Elicitation of moral obligation and self-sacrificing behavior: an experimental study of volunteering to be a bone marrow donor." *Journal of Personality and Social Psychology* 15: 283-293.

——— (1973) "Normative explanations of helping behavior: a critique, proposal, and empirical test." *Journal of Experimental Social Psychology* 9: 349-364.

——— and G. T. CLAUSEN (1970) "Responsibility, norms and helping in an emergency." *Journal of Personality and Social Psychology,* 16: 299-310.

SCHELER, M. (1954) *The Nature of Sympathy.* London: Routledge.

SHAPIRO, D. A. (1969) "Empathy, warmth and genuineness in psychotherapy." *British Journal of Social and Clinical Psychology* 8: 350-361.

SOKOLOV, YE. N. (1963) *Perception and the Conditioned Reflex.* New York: Macmillan.

SPEISMAN, J. C., R. S. LAZARUS, A. M. MORDKOFF, and L. A. DAVISON (1964) "The experimental reduction of stress based on ego defense theory." *Journal of Abnormal and Social Psychology* 68: 367-380.

STOTLAND, E. (1969) "Exploratory studies of empathy." In L. Berkowitz (ed.), *Advances in Experimental Social Psychology,* Vol. 4, New York: Academic Press.

———, S. E. SHERMAN, and K. G. SHAVER (1971) *Empathy and Birth Order.* Lincoln: Univ. of Nebraska Press.

STOTLAND, E. and L. K. CANON (1972) *Social Psychology: A Cognitive Approach.* Philadelphia: W. B. Saunders.

STURUP, G., BOLTON, B., WILLIAMS, D. J., and E. A. CARMICHAEL (1935) "Vasomotor responses in hemiplegic patients. *Brain* 58: 456-468.

SULLIVAN, H. S. (1953) *The Interpersonal Theory of Psychiatry.* New York: W. W. Norton.

TAGIURI, R and L. PETRULLO (1958) *Person Perception and Interpersonal Behavior.* Stanford, Calif.: Stanford Univ. Press.

TEICHNER, W. H. (1965) "Delayed cold-induced vasodilation and behavior." *Journal of Experimental Psychology* 69: 426-432.

TILKER, H. A. (1970) "Socially responsible behavior as a function of observer responsibility and victim feedback." *Journal of Personality and Social Psychology* 14: 95-100.

TOMES, H. (1964) "The adaptation, acquisition and extinction of empathetically mediated emotional responses." *Dissertation Abstracts* 24: 3442-3443.

TRUAX, C. B. (1961) "A scale for the measurement of accurate empathy." *Psychiatric Institute Bulletin* 1, No. 12, Wisconsin Psychiatric Institute, Univ. of Wisconsin.

——— and R. R. CARKUFF (1967) *Toward Effective Counseling and Psychotherapy.* Chicago: Aldine.

WALSTER, E., V. ARONSON, D. ABRAHAMS, and L. ROTTMANN (1966) "Importance of physical attractiveness in dating behavior." *Journal of Personality and Social Psychology* 4: 508-516.

WATSON, D. and R. FRIEND (1969) "Measurement of social-evaluative anxiety." *Journal of Consulting and Clinical Psychology* 33: 448-457.

WEISS, R. F., W. BUCHANAN, L. ALSTATT, and J. P. LOMBARDO (1971) "Altruism is rewarding." *Science* 171: 1262-1263.

WEISS, R. F., J. L. BOYER, J. P. LOMBARDO, and M. H. STICH (1973) "Altruistic drive and altruistic reinforcement." *Journal of Personality and Social Psychology* 25: 390-400.

WINTER, W. D., A. J. FERREIRA, and R. RANSOM (1963) "Two measures of anxiety: a validation." *Journal of Consulting Psychology* 27: 520-524.

WISPÉ, L. G. (1968) "Sympathy and empathy." In D. L. Sills (ed.), *International encyclopedia of the Social Sciences,* Vol. 15. New York: Macmillan.

WRIGHTSMAN, L. S. (1964) "Measurement of philosophies of human nature." *Psychological Reports* 14: 743-751.

——— (1972) *Social Psychology in the Seventies.* Monterey, Calif.: Brooks-Cole.

ZAJONC, R. B. (1968) "Attitudinal effects of mere exposure." *Journal of Personality and Social Psychology* 8: 1-29.

ZIMMER, J. M. and S. ANDERSON (1968) "Dimensions of positive regard and empathy." *Journal of Consulting Psychology* 15: 417-426.

APPENDICES

APPENDIX A: PROCEDURE

The subjects were undergraduates at the University of Washington who were expected to participate in research as part of their introductory course in psychology, although other groups of subjects were used in some studies. Four, five, or six subjects attended each session of the experiment. The subjects, plus one paid assistant trained to act like a subject, sat at three tables, two or three to a table, all facing the front of the room. On the tables before each subject were the apparatus for measuring palmar sweat, a plethysmograph, and a questionnaire lying face down. At the front of the room, with a chair beside it, was a table on which were a diathermy machine and a large separate dial facing the subjects. The diathermy machine was placed so that all the dials and controls could be seen by the subjects. Attached to the table, but out of sight to the subjects, was a button that controlled, in a neighboring room, the event marker on an oscillograph on which vasoconstriction was recorded. At various critical times during the experiment the experimenter pressed the button so that the amount of vasoconstriction could be tied to the events in the experiment. Furthermore, the event recorder was automatically activated when the diathermy machine was turned on or off.

The experimenter introduced the experiment briefly as a study of the "process of social observation as it occurs in small groups with a minimum of information." He then instructed the

AUTHOR'S NOTE: Appendices A, B, and C were originally published, in some instances in different form, in Ezra Stotland, "Exploratory Studies of Empathy," in L. Berkowitz (ed.), *Advances in Experimental Social Psychology,* Vol. 4 (New York, Academic Press, 1969); and in Ezra Stotland, S. E. Sherman, and K. G. Shaver, *Empathy and Birth Order: Some Experimental Explorations* (Lincoln, Nebraska: University of Nebraska Press, 1971). Copyright © 1971 by the University of Nebraska Press. They are reprinted by permission of Academic Press and University of Nebraska Press.

subjects to place the plethysmographs on the thumbs of their nonpreferred hands, telling them that the plethysmographs measured their heartbeats and assuring them that nothing would shock them. Next, after instructing them in the use of the palmar sweat measurement apparatus, he started the first three-minute period of sweat measurement, using the subjects' index fingers. The purpose of this measurement was to provide a baseline for the next period of measuring palmar sweat. During the three-minute period, the experimenter gave the subjects instructions about a questionnaire concerning their opinions of psychological research.

When the three minutes were up, the experimenter continued as follows:

Now, since this is an experiment in social observation, there must necessarily be something for you to observe. And what we are going to have you observe is a demonstration by one of you on this diathermy machine. Before anyone entered the room this afternoon, the laboratory assistant, using a table of random numbers, selected one of the chairs to be the chair of the demonstrator. This position was marked by putting a red X in the lower left-hand corner of the next page of your questionnaire. So could you all turn to the next page of your questionnaires and look in the box for the red X. Now, if you received a red X, that means that you are to be the demonstrator for this session. If you did not receive a red X, that means that you are not to be the demonstrator for this session. You will simply sit in your seat and observe the actual demonstrator as carefully as you can, trying to remember all of your reactions for purposes of filling out the questionnaire at the end.

The paid assistant (now called the demonstrator) then raised his hand and was instructed to sit in the chair beside the table at the front of the room, his back to the other subjects. The experimenter then explained the workings of the diathermy machine and indicated that heat was generated by the two rubber pads lying on the table beside the machine. After turning on the warmup switch, he strapped the demonstrator's hand into the rubber pads. (Needless to say, the machine was not turned on, although all of the lights and dials worked as if it were.) The subjects were then instructed to start another three-minute period of palmar sweat measurement. The experimenter explained that by turning a knob visible to the subjects the machine could be set to give any one of three levels of intensity of heat. He added, "Either it is set at the low level of intensity, which results in a sensation of warmth in the hand of the demonstrator that is quite soothing and quite pleasant, or it is set at the intermediate level, which results in a sensation of heat in the hand of the demonstrator that is neither pleasurable nor painful. Or it is set at a high level of intensity, higher than used by physical therapists, which results in a sensation of pain. However, for a period of 30 seconds, it is neither physiologically nor psychologically damaging. Whichever level is used for a given session is determined by a random device."

Then another, palmar sweat recording was begun. The experimenter then picked up from a deck of cards lying behind the machine a 3-by-5-inch card on which was written "High," "Low," or "Neutral." (The experimenter did not know which of these he would pick up, since the deck had been shuffled in advance by an assistant in order to minimize experimenter effects.) As he picked up the card, the experimenter said, "Now for this session we will use the high (or low or neutral) level of treatment, which most people find painful (or pleasurable or neither painful nor pleasurable)." During the next seven seconds, he adjusted the knobs controlling the level of heat that was supposedly to be administered, the seven seconds being used to give the subjects time to recover from any vasoconstrictions which might have occurred as a result of the announcement of the level of heat to be administered. When the experimenter turned on the heat, the subjects could see the needle on the dial of the diathermy machine as well as the needle on the large adjoining dial, and they could see each needle swinging a distance proportional to the level of heat. When the experimenter turned on the machine for the supposedly high treatment, the demonstrator jerked back and then squirmed moderately in his seat as if he were receiving a painful stimulus; for the mild, pleasurable treatment, he started slightly and then relaxed, slowly moving his hands as if sopping up the warmth; for the neutral condition he hardly gave more than a slight start. The reason for having the demonstrator keep his back to the subjects was that we felt it to be quite impossible for a student assistant to do a convincing job of expressing feelings facially—especially for some 20 sessions. As far as the subjects were concerned, the model kept his back to them because, as the initial instructions stated, the study concerned social perception "with minimal information." The machine was kept "on" for 30 seconds, and when it was shut off, the demonstrator relaxed appropriately and the experimenter told the subjects to fill out the questionnaires. After the palmar sweat recording and the questionnaires were completed, the entire experiment was explained to the subjects.

The subjects' vasconstriction was measured at two points: when the heat level was announced and seven seconds later the machine was supposedly turned on. In the description of the results of the study, these two measures of vasoconstriction will be reported separately.

APPENDIX B:

PHYSIOLOGICAL MEASURES

Because basal skin conductance was measured only in a few studies and because it was not used in the studies described in previous chapters, we will describe here only the methods used for palmar sweating and vasoconstriction.

Palmar Sweating

The measure of palmar sweating used here is a chemical one introduced to psychology by Mowrer (1953). The subject sits at a table with the following apparatus before him: an envelope containing Kleenex and cotton daubers, a jar containing acetone with ferric chloride in solution, and a postal scale with an upright metal piece attached to the back. The top of the metal piece is level with the weighing surface of the scale when it is depressed by one pound of pressure. Attached by Scotch tape to the weighing surface of the scale are one or more sheets of vellum, about two inches square, which have been treated in advance by being soaked in a mixture of tannic acid and water and are therefore impregnated with tannic acid.

The subject administers the measure himself. He is instructed first to take a piece of Kleenex from the envelope and clean off the pad of the finger of his nonpreferred hand that is going to be used. The purpose of this is simply to remove some of the excess dirt and moisture from the finger. Next the subject removes one of the cotton daubers from the envelope, opens the jar of acetone, dips the dauber into the solution, and smears some of the fluid on the pad of the finger he has just dried. Holding that finger in the air, he replaces the cover on the jar. In 20 seconds all of the acetone has evaporated, leaving only the ferric chloride on the pad of the finger. At the end of this 20-second period, the subject presses his finger down on the scale until his finger rests on the tip of the upright metal piece attached to the scale. Thus, he presses his finger with one pound of pressure on the piece of vellum attached to the scale, and he keeps it there for three minutes. During this time, the ferric chloride on the subject's finger dissolves into any perspiration the subject generates. The perspiration with the ferric chloride is absorbed into the vellum and the ferric chloride combines with the tannic acid in the paper to produce an ink. The darkness of the ink fingerprint is proportional to the amount of perspiration. The reason for keeping the pressure at a constant one-pound level for the three-minute period is that the amount of perspiration absorbed by the vellum is also affected by the pressure of the contact. Kuno (1956) reported that the palmar sweat reaction has a very brief latency, but nevertheless, the full impact of palmar sweating either does not occur until a number of seconds after it starts and cannot be fully measured without the three-minute period. The darkness of the ink fingerprint is measured by means of a densitometer. The basic measurement is the difference between the amount of light absorbed by the fingerprint and the amount absorbed by the vellum not touched by the finger.

This measuring procedure is done once as a baseline and then is repeated on the adjoining finger as a critical stimulus is presented. Ferreira and Winter (1963) found that the amount of sweating is consistent among the fingers of the same hand. The difference between the densities of two fingerprints is computed and then is divided by the density of the first, or baseline, fingerprint. The reason for dividing by the baseline density is that the amount of change of palmar sweat from baseline period to stimulus period appears to be roughly proportional to the amount of baseline sweating. If an individual increases in the darkness of his fingerprint from the first to second fingers used, the amount of the increase, in standard units, is his score. If he does not change, his score is zero. If his fingerprint is lighter in the second administration, he is also given a score of zero or no change. The rationale for this procedure is that palmar drying, reflected in the lighter second print, has no psychological meaning; as far as psychological meaning is concerned, there is no such reaction as palmar drying. Any increase in lightness must therefore reflect either unreliability of measurement or a recovery from a palmar sweat reaction which occurred prior to the second fingerprint measure. In either case, the amount of palmar drying can only reflect error variance and is therefore disregarded.

A number of studies have demonstrated the validity of the measurement of palmar sweat as a measure of emotional arousal, particularly of negative emotion. Gladstone (1953) found more palmar sweat after students heard they were about to take an examination than while they were listening to music, more while listening to a mystery than while listening to music, more while talking about birth control than while waiting for an experiment to begin, more while taking a difficult examination than while in an ordinary classroom situation, and so on. Beam (1955) found more palmar sweat before subjects took a doctoral examination, gave an oral report, or appeared in a dramatic production than in a neutral situation. Davis (1957) also found higher palmar sweating during an examination than during a usual classroom situation. Winter, Ferreira, and Ransom (1963) found more palmar sweating while subjects were watching a laboratory film than while they were watching a comedy. They also found more palmar sweat if the experimenter warned students of the dangers from the chemicals used in the measure than if he was casual about the procedure. As in the case of many physiological measures, the relationship of this measurement to pleasure is not clear, but the above studies contain a suggestion that palmar sweating does not reflect pleasure; for example, the findings of Winter et al. show no rise in palmar sweating while the students were watching a comedy.

Vasoconstriction

Vasoconstriction is a very quick reaction consisting of a tightening of the capillaries of the fingers, thus reducing the amount of blood present in the fingers. Vasoconstriction was measured by means of a light plethysmograph placed on the thumb of the subject's nonpreferred hand. The plethysmograph consists of a small bulb with a light which is focused on the subject's finger. On the side of the finger directly opposite the bulb is a photocell sensitive to the amount of light penetrating the finger. Changes in the amount of light penetrating the finger are inversely proportional to changes in the amount of blood in the finger. Accordingly, the pulse in the finger is recorded on an oscillograph connected through an amplifying system to the photocell. With apparatus especially constructed for this series of research projects, it was possible to record the pulse of six subjects simultaneously. Details of the construction and operation of the apparatus are reported elsewhere (Crawford, Stotland, and Shaver, 1967). (The plethysmograph and amplifying equipment were designed and built by Robert Crawford, with some help from Christopher Davis and Tony McKay, Crawford also operated the vasoconstriction apparatus in many of the studies.)

The measure of vasoconstriction is modeled somewhat after the procedure of Davis et al. (1955), and is derived from the oscillographic recording of the pulse. The amplitude of each heartbeat during a specified period is measured, and the average amplitude is found for each heartbeat during that particular time. The first relevant period is the 2.5 seconds before the onset of the critical stimulus; this is the baseline period. The second relevant period is the 7.5 seconds after the critical stimulus. Following Lacey's suggestions (1950) for the construction of an autonomic lability score, a correlation is computed between the baseline amplitude average and the poststimulus average. (The correlations typically range above .90.) This correlation is used in a regression equation to predict poststimulus amplitudes. Each subject's vasoconstriction score is, then, the deviation from his predicted score. The scores in the studies here are reported so that a higher score means more vasoconstriction, although in actuality a lower poststimulus mean amplitude means more vasoconstriction. This procedure does not entail dividing the poststimulus mean amplitude by the baseline amplitude, and thus differs from the procedure used for palmar sweat. Vasoconstriction is handled differently because it was found that, unlike the case with palmar sweat, changes in amplitude are not proportional to the baseline amplitude.

Vasoconstriction appears to be a reflection of both general and emotional arousal. That vasconstriction is a reflection of emotional arousal has been indicated in a number of studies. Nafe and Wagoner (1936) found that if a person put one hand in very cold water, he vasoconstricted in the other hand; the colder the water, the greater the vasoconstriction. Likewise, if the person put one hand in very hot water (above 45 ° C), the hotter the water, the more the vasoconstriction in the other hand. Nafe and Wagoner (1938) found that as the intensity of an electric shock increased, there was a definite relationship between (1) intensity of stimulation, (2) intensity of the pain felt, and (3) the amount of vascular constriction. They also replicated their previous work with hot water and found further that there was a definite relationship between the felt experience of pain and the amount of vasoconstriction. Marquis and Williams (1938) found that people vasoconstricted more if given a strong pin prick than a weak one. Hovland and Riesen (1940) found that the degree of the vasoconstriction increased in direct proportion to the degree of the electric shock the subjects received.

The sensitivity of vasoconstriction to expectations of pain, that is, to cognitive processes, has also been demonstrated. Teichner (1965) found that the threat of receiving a shock shortened the latency and increased the magnitude of vasoconstriction. Furthermore, he found that these effects were greater when the threatened shock was more severe. Sturup, Bolton, Williams, and Carmichael (1935) report that the threat of injury, for example, of a blow in the face, caused vasoconstriction. They also report that when forceps were laid on the skin without an actual pinch being made, "a diminution in the volume of the digits occurred." Vasoconstriction has been found also to reflect nonemotional states of arousal, such as the orienting reflex (Ackner, 1956; Sokolov, 1963). In the present studies it was not possible to differentiate physiologically between the orienting and the emotional reactions. Nevertheless, it is often possible to argue that a difference in vasoconstriction between two experimental conditions reflects a difference in emotional arousal rather than in orienting reflex because the stimulus changes which lead to orienting reflexes are the same in the two conditions. For example, in some studies the other person jerks his arm as if in pain in the presence of people who perceive him as similar to themselves and people who perceive him as different from themselves. Any difference in vasoconstriction between those two conditions can be accounted for in terms of emotional difference, since the jerking of the arm, which causes an orienting reflex, is the same in both conditions. The contrary of vasoconstriction, vasodilation, does not result from any "psychological" procedure, at least as it occurs in the digits. Vasodilations are produced by applying warmth directly to the digits or hand, or they may be a reflection of the recovery phase of an earlier vasoconstriction.

APPENDIX C:

SUBJECTIVE REPORTS

The third type of measure used in these studies was the subjects' reports of their feelings during the critical parts of the experimental period. The reports were obtained immediately after termination of the emotionally arousing stimulus to the person with whom the subject might empathize. The subjects rated their feelings on seven-point or nine-point scales. The questions that were asked differed somewhat from study to study, because it became increasingly apparent through the course of the program that more and more finely discriminating questions were necessary. In general, questions concerned, first, the subjects' feelings of tension or relaxation before, during, and after the other was subjected to emotional stimuli and, second, whether the subjects felt good or bad during these periods. In addition, the subjects in each study were asked about their liking for the other person, their perception of his experiences, their feelings about the experiment, and so on, in order to get a more complete picture of their reactions.

The subjective reports were viewed primarily, but not exclusively, as a way of gaining further clarification of the subjects' physiological reactions. A physiological reaction can be interpreted as indicating a state of arousal, but whether and how the state is empathetic can be determined by an examination of the subjective reports. In addition, because it is not possible to differentiate the various emotions on the basis of physiology alone, further differentiations can be made through these subjective reactions. Thus, if subjects in condition X showed more physiological arousal than those in condition Y, differences between the two conditions were examined by means of the subjective ratings. By using this approach it is possible to learn whether the empathy is simple or contrasting, that is, whether the emotional quality of the observer's reactions is positively or negatively correlated with the other's ostensible emotional reaction. Frequently the quality of the observer's reactions was readily classified as just positive or negative; however, other, more subtle emotional reactions also seemed to be occurring, such as jealousy, envy, and pity. These more subtle states were sometimes reflected in responses to the additional questions that the subjects were asked. But a fuller answer to the question of the more subtle reactions awaits better physiological differentiation of the emotional states.

In some instances of the present research, no difference may be found in the subjective reports between those conditions which do differ in physiological reactions. Our assumption here is that in such instances more subtle questions or more probing would have elicited differences, and empathy may very well have occurred. The basis then becomes much broader for inferring whether it has occurred and which type it is; for example, the experimental context, other relevant data, and so on, contribute information.

As measures of emotional reactions, however, the subjects' reports of their feelings are not given the same status as the physiological measures, for the reason that the subjects may be giving socially desirable descriptions of their own feelings. For example, subjects may perceive that it is socially desirable to respond that one empathizes. But unless their autonomic nervous systems are involved, it is not wise to assume they really have empathized. Of course, it is possible that they were showing their emotions in some physiological system not measured in the studies, but it would not be prudent to simply assume that this was occurring and give the subjective ratings equal status with the physiological.

APPENDIX D: TABLES

Table 2-1: Hierarchy of 36 Categories Used to Map Situations of Empathy

I. Positive (emotion of observed person)
  A. Positive (emotion of observer)
    1. Like (relation between observer and observed)
      a. Physical (area of experience)
      b. Social
      c. Achievement
    2. Similar
      a. Physical
      b. Social
      c. Achievement
    3. Dependence
      a. Physical
      b. Social
      c. Achievement

  B. Negative (emotion of observer)
    1. Like
      a. Physical
      b. Social
      c. Achievement
    2. Similar
      a. Physical
      b. Social
      c. Achievement
    3. Dependence
      a. Physical
      b. Social
      c. Achievement

II. Negative (emotion of observed person)
  (the outline duplicates that under Section I)

Table 2-2: Scale Means and Standard Deviations for Males (N = 224)
and Females (N = 292) and t Tests for Differences in
Means on Empathy

	Total Sample					Validation Study	
	Male		Female			M & F	
Empathy Scale	Mean	SD	Mean	SD	t	Mean	SD
(2) Denial avoidance	17.8	5.0	14.2	4.8	8.07	16.7	5.3
(4) Hostility	12.4	4.0	10.2	3.5	6.49	11.7	4.3
(3) Involvement-concern	19.7	5.0	20.8	4.9	2.51	19.7	6.2
(5) Friend	14.3	3.9	16.9	3.6	7.80	15.0	4.6
(6) Fantasy	7.2	2.4	7.7	2.6	2.25	7.1	2.8

Table 2-3: Number of Subjects in Each of Four Cells of Validation
Study (High and Low Empathy, Male and Female) and
Mean Scores for the Two Positive Empathy Scales

	Involvement-Concern Scale			
	Low		High	
	Male	Female	Male	Female
N	15	12	11	11
Mean score	16.8	13.8	26.0	25.0

	Friend Empathy Scale			
	Low		High	
	Male	Female	Male	Female
N	15	12	11	11
Mean score	10.9	12.8	18.3	20.2

Table 2-4: Significant Correlations between Empathy Scales and
Other Personality Scales (Sarason and Ganzer, 1958)
(All correlations are significant $p < .01$.) (N = 516)

| | Empathy Scales | | | | |
	Denial-Avoidance	Hostility	Involvement-Concern	Friend	Fantasy
Attitudinal hostility		+.25			
Test anxiety					
Hostility		+.23			
Need achievement					
Low defensiveness		−.24	−.17		
Low social desirability		−.17	−.17		
General anxiety	−.20			+.16	
Lack of protection (insecurity in early life)		+.18	+.21		
Anxiety when hostile	−.31		+.25	+.25	+.19
Behavioral hostility		+.20			

Table 2-5: Factor I
            Percentage of Total Variance Accounted for: 11.55
            Percentage of Common Variance Accounted for: 24.96

Loading	Mapping	Number	
.65	22+	34	I become upset watching movies on war and killing.
.63	8+	41	For some reason I usually feel good when my boss does even if it makes no direct difference to me.
.63	23+	37	I get mad if a fellow student is insulted by a professor.
.62	11+	38	I must admit at times I have not been pleased when a friend made a good impression at a party.
.59	29+	39	There are certain people I dislike so much that I am inwardly pleased when they are catching it for something they have done.
.58	22+	35	I have often tried to imagine just how a person who is always hungry must feel.
.54	23—	40	I feel other people ought to take care of their own problems themselves.
.53	Sp+	30	Many times I have felt so close to someone else's difficulties that it seemed as if they were my own.
.52	Sp+	33	When I watch a good movie, I can very easily put myself in the place of a leading character.
.51	Sp+	31	I probably try more than most people to understand the feelings of others.
.48	Sp+	32	Even when I argue with a person, I try to imagine how he feels about his views.
.48	Sp—	42	I am not more sensitive than the normal person about other people's deep feelings.
.48	22—	36	I have the ability to see an animal hurt without being too disturbed.

Table 2-6: Factor II
Percentage of Total Variance Accounted for: 7.86
Percentage of Common Variance Accounted for: 16.97

Loading	Mapping	Number	
.78	Sp—	23	I seldom get deeply involved in the problems and experiences of others.
.60	Sp—	20	I have the ability to view a situation objectively and not get emotionally involved.
.56	27—	25	It seldom bothered me when my parents worried about things such as money.
.52	22—	36	I have the ability to see an animal hurt without being too disturbed.
.52	88—	42	I am not more sensitive than the normal person about other people's deep feelings.
.53	88—	28	When I see strangers, I almost never try to imagine what they are thinking.
.49	23—	40	I feel other people ought to take care of their own problems themselves.
.42	20—	1	One should not get too involved in other people's problems.
.41	31+	7	I must admit that there have been times I have not been bothered to see a person get injured.

Table 2-7:   Factor III
             Percentage of Total Variance Accounted for: 7.84
             Percentage of Common Variance Accounted for: 16.96

Loading	Mapping	Number	
.72	Sp+	26	When I see a retarded child, I try to imagine how he feels about things.
.63	23+	22	When I meet someone who is very ill emotionally, I wonder how I would feel if I were in his shoes.
.50	24+	26	When I see a very old person, I often wonder how I would feel if I were him.
.52	Sp+	31	I probably try more than most people to understand the feelings of others.
.47	Sp+	30	Many times I have felt so close to someone else's difficulties that it seemed as if they were my own.
.44	TS+	15	I often try to guess what other people are thinking before they tell me.
.41	Sp+	32	Even when I argue with a person, I try to imagine how he feels about his views.
.40	9+	21	It meant more to me than most kids when my father would get praise or recognition for something he did.
.40	3+	14	If a friend gets a good summer job, I am more pleased about it than most people would be.

Table 2-8:   Factor IV
             Percentage of Total Variance Accounted for: 7.31
             Percentage of Common Variance Accounted for: 15.00

Loading	Mapping	Number	
.66	12+	18	Sometimes I am not at all pleased when I hear about a person who got top grades.
.59	15+	8	Sometimes it actually bothers me when I hear of a person like myself getting a really good job.
.55	12+	10	At times I have not been happy when a friend got elected to an office in his group.
.55	36+	3	I am pleased when a person who has beaten me in a game gets beaten himself.
.47	PS−	19	When I disagree with a person, I do not try to feel in my own mind the reason why the person holds an opinion different from mine.
.44	21−	5	If my friends get poor grades, that's their problem.
.42	31+	7	I must admit that there have been times I have not been bothered to see a person get injured.

Table 2-9:   Factor V
             Percentage of Total Variance Accounted for: 6.89
             Percentage of Common Variance Accounted for: 14.89

Loading	Mapping	Number	
.68	2+	9	When a friend becomes engaged or gets married, I am very happy.
.66	2+	2	When a friend becomes engaged or gets married, I am almost as happy as if it were happening to me.
.52	19+	17	I get disturbed more than most people when I see a friend getting hurt.
.50	3+	14	If a friend gets a good summer job, I am more pleased about it than most people would be.
.47	6+	16	When someone wins money on a TV quiz show, I get more excited and happy for them than most people do.
.47	31–	4	I have always been disturbed when I have seen a person get injured.
.42	20+	13	I get very uncomfortable when a friend is embarrassed at a party.

Table 2-10: Factor VI
             Percentage of Total Variance Accounted for: 4.82
             Percentage of Common Variance Accounted for: 10.41

Loading	Mapping	Number	
.76	FS+	6	When I am reading an interesting story or novel, I imagine how I would feel if the events in the story were happening to me.
.68	FS+	12	After acting in a play myself, or seeing a play or movie, I have felt partly as though I were one of the characters.
.55	Sp+	33	When I watch a good movie, I can very easily put myself in the place of a leading character.

Table 4-1: Stepwise Regression, Predicting Palmar Sweat
from all Variables (N = 127)

Variable	r	R	R^2*	F (df) of R	p
Fantasy Scale	.144	.144	2.07	2.67 (1,126)	.11
Identification with Mrs. Reynolds	−.127	.208	4.32	3.97 (2,125)	.05

*Percentage of variance controlled.

Table 4-2: Analysis of Variance of Palmar Sweat with Fantasy Scale
and Self-Rating of Identification with Mrs. Reynolds

Variable	df	MS	F	p
Self-Rating (A)	2	.335	3.85	<.05
Fantasy Scale (B)	2	.440	5.06	<.01
Interaction (A x B)	4	.175	2.02	<.10
Error	117	.087		

Table 4-3: Palmar Sweat for each Level of Fantasy Scale and
Self-Ratings of Identification with Mrs. Reynolds

		Fantasy Scale Scores		
	Self-Placement	3-11	12-13	14-15
Ratings of	Low (1-2)	.281	.397	.770
Self-	Median (3-5)	.323	.270	.398
Placement	High (6-9)	.134	.368	.326

Table 4-4: ANOVA of Palmar Sweat, with Fantasy Scale, Identification
with Mrs. Reynolds' Position and Self-Ratings of Tension
Prior to Her Death (N = 127)

	df	MS	F	p
A. Identification	1	.043	.512	
B. Fantasy	2	.209	2.469	$<.10$
C. Tension	1	.056	.664	
A x B	2	.363	4.291	$<.05$
A x C	1	.138	1.630	
B x C	2	.010	.129	
A x B X C	2	.302	3.579	$<.05$
Error	115	.084		

Table 4-5: Mean Palmar Sweating for Different Levels of Fantasy Scale,
Identification with Mrs. Reynolds, and Self-Rating of
Tension Before her Death

Identification with Mrs. Reynolds	Tension	Fantasy Scale		
		(3-11)	(12-13)	(14-15)
(Not imagine) Low	Low	.310	.328	.526
	High	.092	.348	.642
(Did imagine) High	Low	.140	.329	.338
	High	.547	.375	.260

Table 4-6: ANOVA of Palmar Sweat, with Three Levels of Fantasy
Scale, Three Levels of Hospital Experience, and
Identification as Covariate*

	df	MS	F	p
Fantasy scale	2	.314	3.651	.05
Hospital experience	2	.023	.267	
F x experience	4	.208	2.424	$\sim.055$
Covariate (identification)	1	.405	4.709	.05
Error	108	.086		

*Nine Ss not included in analysis because their responses were not scorable.

Table 4-7: Palmar Sweat for Different Levels of Fantasy Scale and Hospital Experience

Hospital Experience	Fantasy Scale		
	(3-11)	(12-13)	(14-15)
1. (None)	.263	.332	.412
2. (To 8 months)	.038	.327	.575
3. (More than 8 months)	.397	.356	.352

Table 4-8: ANOVA of Palmar Sweat with Sum Contact with Illness and Fantasy Scale (Identification as Covariate) (N = 127)

	df	MS	F	p
Illness	2	.211	2.40	.10
Fantasy scale	2	.295	3.36	.05
Illness x fantasy	4	.020	.23	
Covariate (identification)	1	.414	4.73	.05
Error	117	.087		

Table 4-9: Palmar Sweat for Levels of Fantasy Scale and Contact with Illness

Contact with Illness	Fantasy Scale		
	(3-11)	(12-13)	(14-15)
Low	.206	.283	.410
Medium	.185	.286	.446
High	.363	.442	.479

Table 5-1:   Analyses of Variance for Fantasy Scale x Birth Order
x Week of Observation x Family Death

	df	Percentage of Time in Room		Percentage of Time in Hall	
		MS	F	MS	F
Fantasy scale	2	904.1	3.118*	188.6	2.430
Birth order	1	1480.6	5.107***	1.0	
Week of observation	1	429.7	1.482	665.5	8.573***
Family death	1	26.9		68.0	
Fantasy x B.O.	2	183.5		118.4	1.525
Fantasy x W.O.	2	118.6		45.4	
Fantasy x F.D.	2	145.8		3.0	
B.O. x W.O.	1	129.9		7.6	
B.O. x F.D.	1	767.0	2.645	4.2	
W.O. x F.D.	1	914.3	3.154*	39.2	
Fantasy x B.O. x W.O.	2	502.1	1.732	75.5	
Fantasy x B.O. x F.D.	2	27.8		.4	
Fantasy x W.O. x F.D.	2	136.1		142.1	1.831
B.O. x W.O. x F.D.	1	1580.9	5.453**	590.5	7.608***
Fantasy x B.O. x W.O. x F.D.	2	849.4	2.930*	446.5	5.753***
Error	51	289.8		77.6	

*p $<$.10 (1,50) = 2.84   **p $<$.05 (1,50) = 4.03   ***p $<$.01 (1,50) = 7.17
        (2,50) = 2.44   (2,50) = 3.18   (2,50) = 5.06

Table 5-1 (Continued):

	Percentage of Time at Nursing Station		Percentage of Time Interacting		Percentage of Time Interacting in Hallway	
	MS	F	MS	F	MS	F
Fantasy scale	247.1		187.8	3.583**	102.5	5.763***
Birth order	917.9	3.594*	58.9	1.124	8.6	
Week of observation	11.2		580.6	11.079***	135.4	17.613***
Family death	88.9		310.1	5.918***	231.7	13.027***
Fantasy x B.O.	34.5		186.7	3.562**	62.8	3.532**
Fantasy x W.O.	18.1		73.9	1.411	15.0	
Fantasy x F.D.	21.0		42.7		34.1	1.921
B.O. x W.O	2.6		.1		17.5	
B.O. x F.D.	325.0	1.272	97.1	1.853	38.4	2.158
W.O. x F.D.	879.8	3.445*	64.5	1.231	34.0	1.911
Fantasy x B.O. x W.O.	126.7		73.5	1.403	1.3	
Fantasy x B.O. x F.D.	169.7		38.7		35.6	2.00
Fantasy x W.O. x F.D.	119.1		22.1		9.9	
B.O. x W.O. x F.D.	69.4		45.2		86.9	4.886**
Fantasy x B.O. x W.O. x F.D.	267.6	1.048	30.1		28.9	1.629
Error	255.3		52.4		17.7	

*p < .10 (1,50) = 2.84   **p < .05 (1,50) = 4.03   ***p < .01 (1,50) = 7.17
        (2,50) = 2.44   (2,50) = 3.18   (2,50) = 5.06

Table 5-2: Nursing Student Behavior Analyzed by Fantasy Scale,
Birth Order, Week of Observation, and Family Death

5-2A: Percentage Time in Patient's Room

Week	F.D.	Fantasy (FO)			Fantasy (LB)		
		(3-11)	(12-13)	(14-15)	(3-11)	(12-13)	(14-15)
(1-4)	No	78.0	63.3	31.0	66.0	63.2	74.3
	Yes	74.5	62.0	65.5	75.0	75.0	64.0
(5-8)	No	81.0	68.7	86.0	82.0	83.2	56.0
	Yes	66.5	39.0	48.0	92.5	73.8	81.0

5-2B: Percentage Time in Hall

Week	F.O.	Fantasy (FO)			Fantasy (LB)		
		(3-11)	(12-13)	(14-15)	(3-11)	(12-13)	(14-15)
(1-4)	No	8.3	11.6	32.6	8.6	19.7	7.8
	Yes	10.0	14.0	22.5	25.0	14.1	26.5
(5-8)	No	4.6	9.5	5.6	13.6	4.8	19.5
	Yes	9.5	13.0	20.0	3.0	13.4	2.0

5-2C: Percentage Time at Nurses' Station

Week	F.D.	Fantasy (FO)			Fantasy (LB)		
		(3-11)	(12-13)	(14-15)	(3-11)	(12-13)	(14-15)
(1-4)	No	14.0	25.0	36.0	25.3	17.2	17.2
	Yes	15.5	24.0	12.0	.0	11.8	9.0
(5-8)	No	13.6	21.2	8.3	4.4	11.4	23.0
	Yes	23.0	25.5	32.0	4.5	12.4	17.0

5-2D: Percentage Time Interacting with Others

Week	F.O.	Fantasy (FO)			Fantasy (LB)		
		(3-11)	(12-13)	(14-15)	(3-11)	(12-13)	(14-15)
(1-4)	No	1.0	5.3	14.6	.6	13.2	3.2
	Yes	7.0	9.0	28.0	8.0	14.1	13.0
(5-8)	No	.6	1.2	.6	4.0	.4	5.5
	Yes	3.5	4.0	16.0	1.5	2.8	.0

5-2E: Percentage Time Interacting with Others in Hallways

Week	F.D.	Fantasy (FO)			Fantasy (LB)		
		(3-11)	(12-13)	(14-15)	((3-11)	(12-13)	(14-15)
(1-4)	No	.6	3.0	6.6	.3	6.2	2.2
	Yes	2.0	6.6	16.0	8.0	8.6	11.5
(5-8)	No	.6	.2	.6	3.4	.4	4.5
	Yes	1.5	4.0	16.0	1.0	2.4	.0

5-2F: Number of Entries in Each Cell (N = 75)

Week	F.D.	Fantasy (FO)			Fantasy (LB)		
		(3-11)	(12-13)	(14-15)	(3-11)	(12-13)	(14-15)
(1-4)	No	3	3	3	3	4	8
	Yes	2	3	2	1	6	2
(5-8)	No	3	4	3	5	5	2
	Yes	2	2	1	2	5	1

Table 7-1: Correlations between Empathy Scale and Views
            of Human Nature[1]

Variable	Correlation	Significance
Trustworthiness	.06	.31
Strength of will and rationality	.02	.44
Altruistic, unselfish	.27	.02
Independent	.09	.24
Complex	.07	.29
Variable	.30	.01
Favorability of human nature	.15	.13
Mutiplexity	.24	.03
Mach IV	−.02	.44

[1] $N = 62$.

  Data collected in collaboration with D. Nebeker.

Table 7-2: Correlations between Empathy and Other Individual
            Difference Variables*

	IE	Soc. Des.	Soc. Anx.	Birth O.	Sex
Empathy	−.08	−.06	.16	.11	−.09
IE		−.21	.27	−.14	.07
SD			−.04	.04	−.33
Soc. Anx.				−.26	−.06
Birth O.					.17

*n = 44: One subject did not complete the IE, SD, and SA scale.

Table 7-3: Correlations between the Dependent Variables and
Empathy and Other Individual Difference Variables*

Scales	Dependent Variables		
	Similar IJS	Dissimilar IJS	Difference (S-D)
Empathy	.132	−.275**	.301**
IE	−.168	−.029	−.088
SD	.266	−.044	.208
SA	.161	−.180	.243
BO	.143	.088	.024
Sex	.252	.138	.057

*Correlations for empathy, birth order, and sex based on 45 subjects; other correlations based on 44 subjects.
** $p < .05$.

Table 7-4: Analysis of Variance of Evaluations of Dissimilar Others

Source	Sum of Squares	d.f.	Mean Square	F	p
Birth order (A)	6.67	1	6.67	1.53	
Empathy (B)	21.56	2	10.78	2.47	.10
A X B	21.19	2	10.59	2.43	.10
Error	169.89	39	4.36		

Cell Means and Ns (in parentheses)

Subjects	Empathy		
	Low	Moderate	High
First and only	5.83 (6)	7.57 (7)	5.75 (4)
Later born	8.80 (5)	7.15 (13)	5.70 (10)

Table 7-5: Correlations between Empathy and Dependent Variables
Performed Separately for Birth Order Groups

Subjects	N	Dependent Variables		
		Similar IJS	Dissimilar IJS	Difference
First and only	17	.229	.128	.033
Later born	28	.073	−.538*	.488*

*p < .01, two-tailed, 26 d.f.

Table 7-6: Revised 12-Item Empathy Scale in Process of Validation by Disbrow et al. (1977)

Item	Source
1. If my friends get poor grades, that's their problem.	Factor 4 (Hostility)
2. Even when I argue with a person, I try to imagine how he feels about his views.	Factor 3 (Involvement-Concern)
3. When someone wins money on a TV quiz show, I often imagine how I would feel if I were that person.	Factor 6 (Fantasy) (rewritten)
4. Sometimes I'm not at all pleased when I hear about a person who gets top grades.	Factor 4 (Hostility)
5. When I disagree with a person, I do not try to feel in my own mind the reason why the person holds an opinion different from mine.	Factor 4 (Hostility)
6. I must admit that there have been times I have not been bothered to see a person get injured.	Factor 2 (Denial-Avoidance)
7. I feel other people ought to take care of their own problems themselves.	Factor 2 (Denial-Avoidance)
8. When I watch a movie, I often imagine how I would feel if I were that person.	Factor 6 (Fantasy) (rewritten)
9. When I see a very old person, I often wonder how I would feel if I were he.	Factor 3 (Involvement-Concern)
10. When a friend becomes engaged or gets married, I am very happy.	Factor 5 (Friend)
11. When I am reading an interesting story, I imagine how I would feel if I were in the same situation as the people in the story.	Factor 6 (Fantasy) (rewritten)
12. One should not get too involved in other people's problems.	Factor 2 (Denial-Avoidance)

Table 8-1: Mean Empathy Score as Function of Sex and Sex-Type[1]

Sex-Type	Male	Female
Sex-typed	12.098 (41)	11.927 (41)
Androgynous	11.296 (27)	12.568 (37)
Opposite sex-typed	13.111 (9)	13.292 (24)

[1]Group N in parentheses.

Table 8-2: Summary of ANOVA: Empathy as Function of Sex and Sex-Type

Source	df	MS	F
Sex (a)	1	6.18	1.18
Sex-type (B)	2	22.83	4.36*
A x B	2	6.39	1.22
Error	173	5.23	

*$p < .05$.

INDEX

ABOUT THE AUTHORS

EZRA STOTLAND is Professor of Psychology and Director of the Society and Justice Program at the University of Washington, Seattle. A Ph.D. in social psychology (University of Michigan, 1953), Dr. Stotland has held many academic and professional appointments and honors. He is a past President of the Society for the Psychological Study of Social Issues and a consultant with the National Science Foundation. His publications include *Life and Death of a Mental Hospital* (with A. L. Kobler) Seattle: University of Washington Press, 1965; *Psychology of Hope: An Integration of Experimental, Social, and Clinical Approaches* (San Francisco: Jossey-Bass, 1969); *Empathy and Birth Order: Some Experimental Explorations* (with S. E. Sherman and K. G. Shaver) Lincoln, Nebraska: University of Nebraska Press, 1971; and *Social Psychology: A Cognitive Approach* (with L. K. Cannon) Philadelphia, Pennsylvania: Saunders, 1972.

KENNETH E. MATHEWS, Jr. is an Affiliate Assistant Professor of Psychology at the University of Washington and the Senior Researcher and Evaluator for the City of Seattle Law and Justice Planning Office. A Ph.D. from the University of Washington, Seattle, Dr. Mathews has been particularly interested in the study of empathy, helping behavior, and the criminal justice system.

STANLEY E. SHERMAN holds a Ph.D. from the University in Washington, Seattle and has a dual appointment as Associate Professor of Psychology at the California State College, Stanislaus and as Adjunct Professor of Applied Psychology at the Eastern Washington State University at Cheney. Dr. Sherman also functions as a psychotherapist and clinical consultant. He is the author of *Empathy and Birth Order: Some Experimental Explorations* (with K. G. Shaver and E. Stotland) Lincoln, Nebraska: University of Nebraska Press, 1971.

ROBERT O. HANSSON is an Assistant Professor of Psychology at the University of Tulsa, Oklahoma. He holds a Ph.D. in social psychology from the University of Washington, Seattle (1973). Dr. Hansson's published articles in scholarly journals cover a wide range of psychological topics.

BARBARA Z. RICHARDSON is a social psychologist and writer in Seattle, Washington. She has been Managing Editor of the *Bulletin* of the Washington State Division of Mental Health and a Lecturer in Psychology at the University of Washington, where she received her Ph.D. in psychology in 1964. Her articles on psychology and other subjects have appeared in newspapers and magazines in the Pacific Northwest.